MIX
Papier aus verantwortungsvollen Quellen
Paper from responsible sources
FSC® C105338

Heiko Schmolke

The Low Interest Rate Policy of the European Central Bank

Are European Savers being expropriated?

Anchor Academic
Publishing

Schmolke, Heiko: The Low Interest Rate Policy of the European Central Bank. Are European Savers being expropriated?, Hamburg, Anchor Academic Publishing 2017

Buch-ISBN: 978-3-96067-119-0
PDF-eBook-ISBN: 978-3-96067-619-5
Druck/Herstellung: Anchor Academic Publishing, Hamburg, 2017

Bibliografische Information der Deutschen Nationalbibliothek:
Die Deutsche Nationalbibliothek verzeichnet diese Publikation in der Deutschen Nationalbibliografie; detaillierte bibliografische Daten sind im Internet über http://dnb.d-nb.de abrufbar.

Bibliographical Information of the German National Library:
The German National Library lists this publication in the German National Bibliography. Detailed bibliographic data can be found at: http://dnb.d-nb.de

All rights reserved. This publication may not be reproduced, stored in a retrieval system or transmitted, in any form or by any means, electronic, mechanical, photocopying, recording or otherwise, without the prior permission of the publishers.

Das Werk einschließlich aller seiner Teile ist urheberrechtlich geschützt. Jede Verwertung außerhalb der Grenzen des Urheberrechtsgesetzes ist ohne Zustimmung des Verlages unzulässig und strafbar. Dies gilt insbesondere für Vervielfältigungen, Übersetzungen, Mikroverfilmungen und die Einspeicherung und Bearbeitung in elektronischen Systemen.

Die Wiedergabe von Gebrauchsnamen, Handelsnamen, Warenbezeichnungen usw. in diesem Werk berechtigt auch ohne besondere Kennzeichnung nicht zu der Annahme, dass solche Namen im Sinne der Warenzeichen- und Markenschutz-Gesetzgebung als frei zu betrachten wären und daher von jedermann benutzt werden dürften.

Die Informationen in diesem Werk wurden mit Sorgfalt erarbeitet. Dennoch können Fehler nicht vollständig ausgeschlossen werden und die Diplomica Verlag GmbH, die Autoren oder Übersetzer übernehmen keine juristische Verantwortung oder irgendeine Haftung für evtl. verbliebene fehlerhafte Angaben und deren Folgen.

Alle Rechte vorbehalten

© Anchor Academic Publishing, Imprint der Diplomica Verlag GmbH
Hermannstal 119k, 22119 Hamburg
http://www.diplomica-verlag.de, Hamburg 2017
Printed in Germany

Management Summary

This study analyzed the development of inflation-adjusted interest rates of selected asset classes and countries within the sphere of influence of the European Central Bank. Long-term interest rates with a maturity of 10 years, bank interest rates on deposits with an agreed maturity of over one and up to two years, and a return on national share price indices of Germany, Spain, and Luxembourg are studied. The study shows that different factors must be implicated within a critical evaluation. The statement, that savers are expropriated cannot be confirmed essentially. The study also found that the development of inflation-adjusted interest rates varies considerably among the selected countries. Moreover, the monetary policy measures which are implemented in the wake of the latest financial crisis by the European Central Bank are described. Risks and opportunities that emerge in the context of these programs are evaluated. The study concludes, that the European Central Bank is exposed to limitations in regard to an expansion of further measures and raises the question to what extent the policy has to bear additional responsibility.

Table of Contents

1. **Introduction** 1
   - 1.1. Problem Statement and Objective 1
   - 1.2. Approach 3
2. **Monetary Theory** 5
   - 2.1. On Money 7
   - 2.2. Inflation 14
   - 2.3. Interest Rates 25
   - 2.4. Monetary Policy 29
   - 2.5. Transmission Mechanism 38
   - 2.6. Financial Repression 41
3. **The European Central Bank** 44
   - 3.1. History and Structure 44
   - 3.2. Principles and Objectives 46
   - 3.3. Monetary Policy Instruments 50
4. **Interest Levels and Savings Behavior** 58
   - 4.1. Nominal Interest Rate 58
   - 4.2. Real Interest Rate 60
   - 4.3. Savings Behavior 62
5. **The Development of Yield Levels** 64
   - 5.1. Methodology of the Empirical Study 68
   - 5.2. The Development of Yield Levels in Germany 70
   - 5.3. The Development of Yield Levels in Spain 74
   - 5.4. The Development of Yield Levels in Luxembourg 76
   - 5.5. Results of the Empirical Study 78
6. **Implications and Evaluation** 81
   - 6.1. Risks 81
   - 6.2. Opportunities 83
   - 6.3. Possibilities and Limitations of the ECB 84
7. **Conclusion** 86

Bibliography 88

Appendices 109

List of Abbreviations

ABSPP	Asset-backed securities purchase program
AfD	Alternative für Deutschland
APP	Asset purchase program
Bln	Billion
BOE	Bank of England
BOJ	Bank of Japan
CBPP	Covered bond purchase program
CPI	Consumer price index
CSPP	Corporate Sector Purchase Program
e.g.	For example
EC	European Commission
ECB	European Central Bank
ECJ	European Court of Justice
EEC	European Economic Community
EFSF	European Financial Stability Facility
EMU	Economic and Monetary Union
ESCB	European System of Central Banks
ESM	European Stability Mechanism
EU	European Union
FAZ	Frankfurter Allgemeine Zeitung
FED	Federal Reserve System
ff.	Following pages
FOMC	Federal Open Market Commitee
GDP	Gross domestic product
HICP	Harmonized index of consumer prices
ibid.	Ibidem
IPI	Import price index
LTRO	Longer-term refinancing operations
MFI	Monetary financial institution
MRO	Main refinancing operations
NCB	National Central Bank
OECD	Organisation for Economic Cooperation and Development

p.	Page
pp.	Pages
PPI	Producer price index
PSPP	Public sector purchase program
QE	Quantitative easing
resp.	respectively
SMP	Securities markets program
SNB	Swiss National Bank
TFEU	Treaty on the Functioning of the European Union
TLTRO	Longer-term refinancing operations
U.S.	United States
USA	United States of America
Vol.	Volume
XPI	Export price index

List of Figures

Figure 1:
The Principle of money creation 12

Figure 2:
The Keynesian cross 15

Figure 3:
Monthly percentage change of the U.S. M2 and the U.S. CPI
with corresponding moving average 18

Figure 4:
Weights of the main product groups in the euro area HICP 22

Figure 5:
Development of inflation of the euro area, Japan, and USA,
based on a monthly basis 24

Figure 6:
General objectives of monetary policy 30

Figure 7:
Main transmission channels of monetary policy decisions 41

Figure 8:
Timeline of selected key events of the foundation of the ECB 44

Figure 9:
Monetary policy strategy of the euro area 50

Figure 10:
Key interest rates issued by the ECB 52

Figure 11:
Volume of open market operations, deposit facility,
and minimum reserves held with the ECB 53

Figure 12:
Holdings by the ECB of securities held for monetary policy purpose 57

Figure 13:
Key interest rates of the euro area, USA, Japan 59

Figure 14:
The development of inflation, the MRO lending rate,
and the real interest rate within the euro area 62

Figure 15:
Structure of gross financial assets of selected countries 63

Figure 16:
Development of inflation in Germany, Spain and
Luxembourg from 1999-2016 65

Figure 17:
Development of real interest rates in Germany 71

Figure 18:
Development of real interest rates in Spain 74

Figure 19:
Development of real interest rates in Luxembourg 76

List of Tables

Table 1:
Definitions of U.S. monetary aggregates 8

Table 2:
Definitions of euro area monetary aggregates 9

Table 3:
Classification of interest rates based on capital forms 27

Table 4:
Overview of selected interest rates within the euro area 28

Table 5:
Selection criteria for the chosen countries and their placements
within the euro area 64

Table 6:
Correlation of yield levels in Germany with the MRO lending rate 72

Table 7:
Correlation of yield levels in Germany with asset purchase programs
by the ECB 73

Table 8:
Correlation of yield levels in Spain with the MRO lending rate 75

Table 9:
Correlation of yield levels in Spain with asset purchase programs
by the ECB 75

Table 10:
Correlation of yield levels in Luxembourg with the MRO lending rate 77

Table 11:
Correlation of yield levels in Luxembourg with asset purchase programs
by the ECB 78

Table 12:
Means and standard deviation of the evaluated inflation-adjusted interest rates ... 79

1. Introduction

Since the collapse of the U.S. investment bank Lehman Brothers in 2008 and the subsequent global financial and economic crisis, all major central banks have undertaken unconventional measures to protect production and real economy (Global Investor 2016; Smith 2014). The first intervention came from the central bank of the United States, the Federal Reserve (FED), which lowered key interest rates to almost zero in 2007, followed by reciprocal currency agreements with other major central banks and the purchase of large amounts of U.S. Treasury securities and mortgage-backed securities (Wheelock 2010, pp. 91 ff.). A noteworthy monetary policy measure in regard to the changed global economic conditions since 2007 was the implementation of negative key interest rates of major central banks in the Western hemisphere. In July 2009, the Swedish National Bank cut a key interest rate to -0.25 percent, followed by the Danish National Bank in December 2012, the European Central Bank (ECB) in June 2014, the Swiss National Bank (SNB) in December 2014, and finally even Japan in January 2016 (euro|topics 2009; Romeo 2016, p. 25). Since the implementation of negative key interest rates, economists, politicians, scientists, and media have discussed the topic with various degrees of seriousness, emotion and polemic. The underlying key question however is: What consequences will the people face in regard to these monetary policy decisions? This research study therefore shall play its part to answer this question scientifically.

1.1. Problem Statement and Objective

In early spring of 2016, German media, economists and politicians criticized the ECB's low nominal interest rate policy more intensely than ever before. This was at a time, when the ECB announced an expansion of the previous quantitative easing by its corporate sector purchase program (CSPP) to boost the persistently low inflation (ECB 2016a). Influential and highly respected politicians were stated at that time with comments that are at least questionable and partially even irresponsible:

> *"Schäuble: Monetary policy jointly responsible for success of AfD"*
> (FAZ 2016)[1]

---

[1] „Schäuble: Geldpolitik mitverantwortlich für Erfolge der AfD" (FAZ 2016, translation by author).

> *"European Central Bank in the critique, Bavaria's Finance Minister rails: "German savers are expropriated sneakingly.""*
>
> (FOCUS-MONEY 2016)[2]

Reputable newspapers, as well as the yellow press jumped the gun and started a campaign against the policy of the ECB and its president Mario Draghi in person:

> *"[...] Mario Draghi is just ruining Europe's future."*
>
> (SZ 2016)[3]

> *"[...] The deliberate expropriation of savers in Europe is pushed ahead. [...] (and [author's note]) It is time that the ECB comes to his senses and no longer tries, regardless of losses, to enforce their own interests like the North Korean regime."*
>
> (n-tv 2016)[4]

In face of unprecedented negative media coverage and political opposition, it seems especially important to analyze and examine this topic with scientific rigor. Or we expose ourselves to populism dictating the debate. It is of great value to society to make macro economical decisions as comprehensible as possible. Certain is, that an alteration of key interest rates will influence the national economy. There is plenty of empirical evidence that the value of interest rates impacts savings behavior of people (Mankiw 2011, p. 462; Benassy-Quere et al. 2010, p. 243). However, there is a lack of understanding to what extent negative interest rates will influence the saving behavior. In May 2015, the ECB published a paper where they explained their accommodating policy and tried to foster trust of the public in their decisions (Bindseil 2015). A plenty of theoretical analysis have been published in regard to the topic of negative interest rates and their potential risk but also possible opportunities (Romeo 2016, Greeley et al. 2015; Platt 2015).

---

[2] „Europäische Zentralbank in der Kritik, Bayerns Finanzminister wettert: "Die deutschen Sparer werden schleichend enteignet"" (FOCUS-MONEY 2016, translation by author).
[3] „[...] Mario Draghi ist gerade dabei, Europas Zukunft zu ruinieren." (SZ 2016, translation by author).
[4] „[...] Die vorsätzliche Enteignung der Sparer in Europa wird weiter forciert. (und [Anm. d. Verf.]) Es ist an der Zeit, dass die EZB zur Vernunft kommt - und nicht länger versucht, wie ein nordkoreanisches Regime ohne Rücksicht auf Verluste ihre eigenen Interessen durchzusetzen."
(n-tv 2016, translation by author).

Because the subject is still relatively recent, there is a lack of scientific and empirical investigation in the context of real influence and correlation of the current level of interest rates and yield levels of asset classes.

This research therefore will try to answer central questions to understand the context of low and negative interest rates and the return of savers: How was the development of yield levels of selected asset classes from 1999-2016 by taking into account the real interest rate within the sphere of influence of the European Central Bank? Are the yield levels declining? Are depositors really be expropriated slowly, as political parties argued? What role play the selected asset classes regarding a critical evaluation of the aforementioned concerns?

1.2. Approach

This study consists of a theoretical part and an empirical analysis. Within the theoretical treatise, the main theoretical approaches of monetary theory are described. These include the principles of money creation, inflation, the fundamentals and mechanisms of monetary policy and their transmission mechanisms. In order to examine contemporary mainstream economics critical, current empirical studies and findings are also taken into account. Since the monetary policy decisions of the ECB play a major role in the subsequent empirical analysis, the ECB is described after the treatise of the theoretical basis. In doing so, the principles, objectives, and monetary policy instruments of the ECB are shown in more detail. Main subject of the empirical study are interest rates. For this reason, the concepts of nominal and real interest rates are described prior to the empirical study. This includes also a brief outline of the savings behavior of selected countries in Europe. The subsequent empirical study concerns the development of selected asset classes and countries in Europe. The selected interest rates can be regarded as reference rates for short and long term asset classes, whereat the stock market is also taken into account. The countries concerned are Germany, Spain, and Luxembourg. By calculating the inflation-adjusted interest rate of the mentioned asset classes, it is intended to provide the most realistic view on the developments and current levels of the analyzed interest rates. An additional correlation evaluation of the interest rates with the key interest rate is subsequently used to confirm theoretical approaches, respectively help to identify additional mechanism of action in regard of interest rate developments. A final evaluation of possible implications regarding risks and opportunities of the current monetary policy of the ECB completes the study.

2. Monetary Theory

The following chapter provides the basis for the understanding of monetary policy. It discusses the main theoretical approaches, which deal with the monetary phenomena of monetary policy measures. It will also try to examine these theoretical approaches critical, based on current empirical studies and findings.

Monetary theory is the discipline which deals with the nature, functions, value, and effects of money. During the traditional monetary theory between the 19th and 20th century, the majority opinion was that the goods economic (real) and the money economy (monetary) sector of the economy were independent of each other (Mankiw 2015, p. 639). In such a condition, money can be considered as neutral and a change in the stock of money will only have an impact on nominal variables like prices and wages and no impact on real variables, such as employment rate, gross domestic product (GDP), or even consumption. This kind of dichotomy was first left behind by John Maynard Keynes (1883 - 1946), who published in his 'General Theory of Employment, Interest and Money' in 1936 an economic concept, that based on a simultaneous analysis of real (income and employment) and monetary (money supply and interest) variables (Keynes 1936, p. 293). In the following years, further schools of thought were formed and they are still present today. The differentiation of the prevalent theory after the 1960s was mainly reasoned by the finding, that the years earlier publicized context between unemployment rate and the rate of change of money wage rates, which later gave way to the inflation rate, could not be observed in reality during the 1970s and 1980s. The mentioned context is known as Phillips curve (Mankiw 2015, p. 771 ff.). Between the 1960s and 1970s, Milton Friedman promoted his concept, known as the monetarism school, where he postulated a key-context between money supply and inflation and gave the Phillips curve a different interpretation. From his point of view, the regulation of the money supply is the most important key variable to control economic processes, so 'money matters' (Handa 2002, p. 48).

Today, Keynesian economics and monetarism are still the two main macroeconomic models, which influence fiscal decisions, where although both scientific trends have been developed further. New Keynesian economics combines the methodical progress of the school of monetarism with the school of new classical macroeconomics and is nowadays an international macroeconomic mainstream. The before-mentioned school of thoughts incorporates all available information in the expectation formation. This theory states, that monetary policy has no effect on economy, unless monetary policy was unpredictable. The school of new classical macroeconomics is also based on the concept of a perfect neutrality of money (Handa 2002, p. 474). One modern theory, that combines central elements from the new classical macroeconomics with elements from Keynesian macroeconomics is the new neoclassical synthesis and is more or less the theoretical foundation for much of contemporary mainstream economics and the theoretical basis for decision making of almost every major central bank (Scarth 2016, New neoclassical synthesis). The new neoclassical synthesis involves assumptions like *"[...] intertemporal optimization, rational expectation processes, monopolistic competition, and costly price adjustment in a dynamic price setting while restoring the utility of monetary policy to fight economic fluctuations."* (Barbaroux 2013, p. 15).

However, different perspectives on economics exist still today, which are relevant or been discussed seriously, e.g. whether the supply or demand side of the economy is decisive for fiscal policy. Especially during the global financial crisis in 2007/2008 and the following years, conventional and classical explanations were put into question. Nevertheless, there are crucial relations and elements from the aforementioned macroeconomics school of thoughts that are very relevant for this study. The following bullet points summarize these key elements which can be considered as contemporary (Handa 2002, p. 399; Benchimol 2015, Abstract):

- The classical dichotomy holds in the long-run: Changes in the money supply, or equivalently a change in the interest rate, are neutral.

- The classical dichotomy is not given in the short-run: Changes in the money supply, or equivalently a change in interest rate changes the production, output, and unemployment.

- The neutrality of money holds only in the long-run.

- Monetary policy measures are therefore effective in the short-run.

- High inflation has negative welfare effects.

The enumerated premises are at large the basis for decision-making of every fiscal institution of a technically and economically advanced state. Before financial decisions of relevant institutions can be discussed, it is appropriate to identify key elements and concepts of the monetary theory in more detail.

2.1. On Money

The basis for almost every topic within monetary theory is money. According to Mankiw (2015), money is *"[...] the set of assets in an economy that people regularly use to buy goods and services from other people."* (Mankiw 2015, p. 610). Historically, the emergence of complex human societies is highly correlated to the social habit of using money for transactions. However, there are some more functions to money than its transactional value. The original use of money can be considered as a **medium of exchange**. This refers to a medium or item by which barter processes can be carried out. To value the objects which are subjects of the transaction process, money furthermore has the function as a **unit of account**. It is also used as a scale to post prices and record debts (ibid.). In this context, it serves as a benchmark for the amount of wagework, and goods, respectively services, that can be paid or earned with it as well. The amount of money that someone has corresponds to the share of the national product, he could potentially acquire, if he spends the money. In doing so, the value of a monetary unit is referred to as purchasing power of money (Lipsey, Harbury 1992, pp. 334 ff.). To handle and transfer such purchasing power from the present into the future, money has also the function as a **store of value.** This means that money as an equivalent value for other goods or services can be saved and redeemed at another time and at another place. Therefore, a store of value must be able to retain its value permanently. For this reason, some ancient societies used non-perishable artefacts such as diamonds or gold for this function (Deepashree 2016, p. 4.2). Among economists, the aforementioned functions in bold are the most important ones. Mankiw (2015) adds another function that is also relevant for this study. He uses the word **liquidity**, that can be considered as *"[...] the ease with which an asset can be converted into the economy's medium of exchange."* (Mankiw 2015, p. 611).

Derived from the attributes above, money can be classified into two types. Based on its function as a store of value and the characterization of non-perishability, it must have an intrinsic value. In this a case, it is called **commodity money** and is *"[...] intrinsically useful as an input to production or consumption."* (Durlauf, Blume 2009, p. 27). Gold is the most famous example for this kind of money. It can be used as (commodity) money and it is at the same time an important component within micro technology and industry. The other type of money is characterized by its lack of value. This is the money highly developed societies nowadays use. With this kind of money all the other functions from above can be accomplished most effectively. The central feature of this money is its legality, approved by a decree of a state (Mankiw 2015, p. 612). For this reason, every kind of paper money in the form of a dollar bill or a euro bill, etc. corresponds to this type of money and is called **fiat money**.

Money Supply

People in modern societies have different possibilities to transfer their purchasing power into the future. They deposit their assets in bank accounts, usually in the form of saving deposits, funds, or shares. To handle different types of assets as equivalents to money, national economies define different types of monetary aggregates. Traditionally they are named as $M0$, MB, $M1$, $M2$, $M3$, MZM, where $M0$, $M3$, and MZM are not used constantly by every national economy or major national bank (Brown 1995, p. 748; Dobeck, Elliott 2007, p. 32; Handa 2002, p. 10; Belke, Polleit 2009, p. 60). In general, it can be said, that the money supply is the quantity of money that is available in a national economy at a specific time (Mankiw 2011, p. 626). The following overview provides the definition of the aforementioned aggregates of the two largest central banks in the world, the European Central Bank and the Federal Reserve (CMS Forex 2016):

Monetary Aggregates (FED)	MB	M1	M2	MZM
Currency in circulation and reserve balances	X			
Currency held by the public		X	X	X
Transaction deposits at depository institutions		X	X	X
Savings deposits and small-denomination time deposits of less than $100.000			X	
Retail money market mutual fund shares			X	X
Institutional money funds (money zero maturity)				X

Table 1: Definitions of U.S. monetary aggregates
(Illustration by author, data source: Federal Reserve 2016a, Federal Reserve Bank of St. Louis 2016a)

Since the 1940s the FED publishes data on the money supply, which had started first with currency in circulation, demand deposits, and time deposits, and was enlarged by the aggregates $M1$, $M2$, and $M3$ in 1971. However, since 2006, the Board of Governors stopped publishing the $M3$ monetary aggregate (New York FED 2016).[5]

Monetary Aggregates (ECB)	M1	M2	M3
Currency in circulation	X	X	X
Overnight deposits	X	X	X
Deposits with an agreed maturity up to 2 years		X	X
Deposits redeemable at a period of notice up to 3 months		X	X
Repurchase agreements			X
Money market fund (MMF) shares/units			X
Debt securities up to 2 years			X

Table 2: Definitions of euro area monetary aggregates
(Illustration by author, data source: ECB 2016b)

According to the ECB's definition of euro area monetary aggregates, the narrow aggregate ($M1$), the intermediate aggregate ($M2$), and the broad aggregate ($M3$) vary in regard to their moneyness of the assets included of residents in the EU which are held with monetary financial institutions (MFI), such as banks, building societies, and money market funds located in the euro area. Euro residents that hold liquid assets in other currencies than the Euro, can be close substitutes for Euro-denominated assets and are included into the corresponding aggregates if they are held with MFIs located in the euro area (ECB 2016b).

The definition of monetary aggregates varies among various central banks. This has some very pragmatic reasons, for example the savings behavior of the population, the willingness to take risks, or the dependence on foreign trade and industry of the concerned economy.

---

[5] In November 2005, the FED announced to cease publication of the M3 monetary aggregate by 23rd March 2006, together with large-denomination time deposits, repurchase agreements (RPs), and Eurodollars. According to the Fed, the *"M3 does not appear to convey any additional information about economic activity that is not already embodied in M2 and has not played a role in the monetary policy process for many years."* (Federal Reserve 2006).

Money Creation

The process by which the money supply is increased is the process of money creation. Outside the mainstream economics, there are several processes known and heterodox theories discussed of how money can be created (Bell 2001, pp. 150 ff.; Ryan-Collins et al. 2012, 3.3 ff.). For a more detailed view I refer to the book *"Where Does Money Come From?: A Guide to the UK Monetary and Banking System"* from Ryan-Collins et al. (2012), which is a Create Common publication, and the article of Stephanie Bell (2001) about *"The role of the state and the hierarchy of money"* in the Cambridge Journal of Economics from March 2001. There are two main processes relevant and important for this study. The first process relates to the creation of money by the central bank. The kind of money that is created by this process is also called central bank money or more common monetary base ($M0$). The monetary base consists of cash, that has been circulated by the central bank, and deposits of commercial banks deposited with the central bank. Of particular importance are the deposits of commercial banks with the central bank, because they are used for processing payments and correspond to the obligation of commercial banks to maintain a so called minimum reserve at the central bank (Deutsche Bundesbank 2016a). The minimum reserve was first introduced in the beginning of the 19th century in the U.S. and owes its origin to the security needs of customers. With this reserve, liquidity should be ensured in case of a rush of customers on commercial banks (Lloyd 2006, p. 287). Today there is another important aspect in regard to the requirements of minimum reserves that are explained in more detail under the second process of money creation. To sum up, the minimum reserve, or also required reserve, is the minimum amount of reserves a bank must hold against its checkable deposits as mandated by the central bank (Arnold 2008, p. 259). The ratio of these deposits that must be held in reserve form is called required reserve ratio, or reserve-deposit ratio r_r (ibid.):

$$required\ reserves = r_r \cdot checkable\ deposits$$

Or in general:

R = reserves
D = (checkable) deposits
r_r = reserve-deposit ratio

$$r_r = \frac{R}{D} \quad (2.1.1)$$

Reserves that are held beyond the required amount with the central bank are called excess reserves:

$$excess\ reserves = reserves - required\ reserves$$

Another possibility of central banks to increase or decrease central bank money are open market operations, where central banks purchase or sell securities or bonds to commercial banks. This topic is examined in more detail under chapter 2.4 and 3.3 of this research.

Since the middle of, respectively the end of the 20th century, in Germany and later in other countries in the EU exists another tool to avoid a run on banks in case of bankruptcies or economic crises. This tool is known as deposit insurance or deposit guarantee, where deposits are protected by law to a certain amount per person. In the euro area, it is regulated by EC Directives 94/19/EC. In Germany, this directive is put into practice with the German Deposit Guarantee Act and guaranties 100% of deposits up to a maximum of EUR 100,000 per person in case of bankruptcy of a financial institution (German Deposit Guarantee Act, §8). Therefore, the risk for a run on banks in the mentioned situations is not that likely as in the beginning of the 20th century. For this reason, the proportion of required reserves in developed countries is generally between 1 and 10%.

The height of required reserves can only be determined by central banks and they also use it to stimulate money creation by commercial banks (Arnold 2008, p. 259). This second process is illustrated in figure no. 1, where a starting balance of EUR 100,000 is given and is deposited at the bank, so a fund is placed. This amount appears on the assets side of the balance of the commercial bank. Furthermore, a reserve-deposit ratio is assumed of $r_r = 10\%$. Excluding the required reserve, the bank has now EUR 90,000 in excess reserves on their asset site and still EUR 100,000 on their liabilities site. The amount of EUR 90,000 in excess reserves can be loaned out to another customer, or can be deposited with the central bank. Under normal economic conditions, commercial banks lend these excess reserves out. If another customer receives this amount, in whatever it will be invested, it will appear again on the liabilities site of a bank account again, the same or a different bank, because the money will be paid back into a bank again. Let us assume it is a different bank, which has now EUR 90,000 on the liabilities site and on the asset site EUR 9,000 required reserves and now EUR 81,000 in excess reserves. The described process from above can start again, where the second bank lends out these excess reserves of about EUR 81,000.

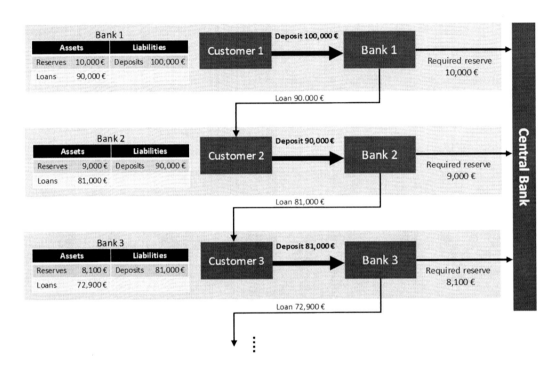

Figure 1: The Principle of money creation
(Illustration by author, random chosen reference parameter)

The described process can be modeled as an infinite geometric series, where the reserve-deposit ratio determines the amount of money creation.

$$money\ supply = 100,000 + 90,000 + 81,000 + 72,900 + \cdots$$
$$= 100,000 \cdot (0.9^0 + 0.9^1 + 0.9^2 + 0.9^3 + \cdots)$$

with the use of a geometric series follows:

$$a \sum_{n=0}^{\infty} q^n = \sum_{n=0}^{\infty} a \cdot q^n = a \cdot \frac{1}{(1-q)}, with\ |q| < 1$$

$$= 100,000 \cdot \left(\frac{1}{1-0.9}\right) = 100,000 \cdot \left(\frac{1}{0.1}\right) = 1,000,000 = M = D \cdot \frac{1}{r_r}$$

Or in general (Mankiw 2003, p. 580 ff.):

M = money supply

C = currency

$B = C + D$ = monetary base

$c_r = \frac{C}{D}$ = currency-deposit ratio

$m = \frac{C+D}{B}$ = money multiplier

$$M = C + D = \frac{C+D}{B} \cdot B = m \cdot B \qquad (2.1.2)$$

The money multiplier m shows the increase in the money supply resulting from a one-Euro increase in the monetary base. According to the aforementioned relations, and if $r_r < 1$, then $m > 1$, can be concluded, that $\Delta M = m \cdot \Delta B$. This mathematical relationship shows, that a fractional-reserve banking system creates money.

Unfortunately, since the beginning of the financial crisis in 2007, the following years have shown, that the macroeconomic doctrine did not worked as expected and the process of the money multiplier collapsed in the USA. This can be reasoned by the quantitative easing program of the FED. The FED started to pay an interest on excess reserves held with the central bank, that was higher than the upper band of the FED Funds Rate. Banks decided to deposit their excess reserves virtually risk-free with the central bank, then lending them out to a certain degree of higher risk (Schmolke 2015, p. 13). Furthermore, recent studies show that consequent interest rate policies and monetary policy purchase programs by the central bank affect the prices and quantities of a range of assets in the economy, including money, more efficiently than a direct control of base or broad money (McLeay et al. 2014, Conclusion). This important finding has influenced the policy of the ECB in recent years, which is shown in more detail in chapter 3 of this research.

The described process of money creation shows, that every deposit of a creditor has an equal amount of liabilities on the debtor-site and thus all credits and debits add up purely logical, balance related, and macroeconomic to zero. In a credit money system, therefore macroeconomically no net financial assets exist, only tangibles or real assets (Schmidt, J. 2012).

2.2. Inflation

A central characteristic of Western economies are their flexible prices. This means that the prices of individual goods are flexible regarding market-based coordination of individual economic plans. This is necessary to enable adjustment processes where factors of production and goods are in an unbalanced state. Flexible prices therefore fulfill allocative purposes and contribute to a market supply in a certain point in time or an entire period (Kampmann, Walter 2013, p. 15). It is problematic if a common increase in the most prices of goods can be observed. Such price level increases may cause a general loss of purchasing power and consumer can buy in total less than before. This phenomenon is called inflation. The opposite, where general price reductions can be observed is called deflation (ibid.). Thus, inflation is a continued and sustainable price level increase, or according to Mankiw and Taylor (2011) *"[...] an increase in the overall level of prices in the economy."* (Mankiw, Taylor 2011, p. 14). There are two relevant approaches to describe the phenomenon of inflation: The monetary inflation theory and the non-monetary inflation theory (Springer Fachmedien Wiesbaden 2013, p. 191). The main relevant for monetary policy measures and this study are the explanation approaches of Keynesianism, monetarism, and new classical macroeconomics.

Keynesian Theory of Inflation

According to this theory, the cause of inflation is demand for goods, or demand pull, which exceeds the level of full employment, and thus causes an inflationary gap (Anderegg 2007, p. 212). This explanation makes use of the Phillips curve, but refers to the inflation rate instead of wage increases within the assessment. The central characteristic of this explanatory approach is the assertion, that an increase in the money supply does not necessarily lead to a proportional change in prices. In other words, the monetary-related demand for goods is not increasing in the same proportion as the quantity of money. This is particularly relevant for a so-called liquidity trap, in which the total additional money supply is absorbed by an increased demand for money. Moreover, the theory also implies that the monetary conditions and the amount of interest rates in the money-market affects the return ratios to the other assets and thus the demand for those assets, until there is an equilibrium. If an increase in the money supply causes a decrease of interest rates in the money markets, an increased demand arises for the substitution of assets for capital goods. Through the resulting multiplier process income increase and consumption increase, and thus a further increase in effective demand. This can cause pricing effects in regard to initial changes in the monetary area. Figure 2 illustrates the theoretical context graphically and the impact of a change in effective demand as well as the emergence of a deflationary, respectively inflationary gap.

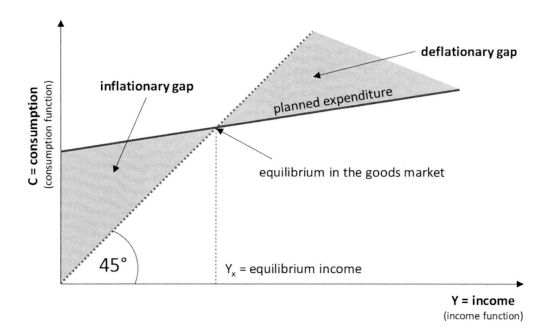

Figure 2: The Keynesian cross
(Illustration by author)

In summary, the theory states that with declining unemployment the national income increases and through this the consumer demand for goods increases more than additional production capacity can be created (Anderegg 2007, p. 213).[6]

Monetary Theory of Inflation

In contrast to the Keynesian theory of inflation, the monetary theory of inflation is geared towards the classical and neoclassical doctrine of monetarily induced inflationary processes (Anderegg 2007, p. 214). Milton Friedman (1912-2006), as a leading representative of monetarism, asserted: *"[...] long-continued inflation is*

---

[6] According to Anderegg (2007) from the University of Cologne, not all correlations could be observed in the euro area between 1999-2005. Although the inflation rate tends to increase with an increasing demand (and vice versa). However, the inflation rate increases only slightly with an increasing level of employment (Anderegg 2007, p. 214).

always and everywhere a monetary phenomenon that arises from a more rapid expansion in the quantity of money than in total output." (Friedman 1974, p. 10)[7].

The basis for all processes described within the monetary theory of inflation is an equation which uses the monetary base, the velocity of money, prices of output, and the quantity of output to describe a ratio. This equation is called 'quantity equation' and can be derived as follows. With:

$$V = \frac{T}{M}$$

where V = velocity of money, which is the rate at which money circulates, e.g. the number of times the average Euro bill changes hand in a certain period, T = value of all transactions, and M = money supply follows:

$$V = \frac{P \cdot Y}{M}$$

where P = price of output, or GDP deflator, Y = quantity of output, or real GDP, and $P \cdot Y$ = value of output, or nominal GDP. Subsequently, the quantity equation follows from the preceding definition of velocity of money (Mankiw 2015, p. 465):

$$M \cdot V = P \cdot Y \qquad (2.2.1)$$

This equation is an identity, which means that the equation is true for all possible parameter values. The monetary theory of inflation, or short 'quantity theory' predicts a one-for-one relation between changes in the money growth rate and changes in the inflation rate. To verify this assumption with the use of the aforementioned equation, some further assumptions are necessary.

If V = constant and exogenous, because it is empirically verifiable that the velocity of money is relatively stable over time, and the growth rate of a product equals the sum of the growth rate, follows:

---

[7] „*This is a bit of an over-simplification, because a fully defensible statement would have to allow for autonomous changes in velocity, i.e., in the demand for real balances, and would have to specify the precise definition of 'money'. But I know of no case in which these qualifications are of critical importance.*" Note from Milton Friedman (Friedman 1974, p. 17).

$$\frac{\Delta M}{M} + \frac{\Delta V}{V} = \frac{\Delta P}{P} + \frac{\Delta Y}{Y}$$

$$\text{if } V = const. \Rightarrow \frac{\Delta V}{V} = 0 \Rightarrow \frac{\Delta M}{M} = \frac{\Delta P}{P} + \frac{\Delta Y}{Y}$$

With $\pi = \frac{\Delta P}{P}$, which denotes the inflation rate, follows (Mankiw, Taylor 2006, p. 616):

$$\pi = \frac{\Delta M}{M} - \frac{\Delta Y}{Y} \qquad (2.2.2)$$

Furthermore, it can be shown, that if the velocity of money is constant, the nominal GDP is mainly determined by the money supply:

$$\text{if } V = const. \Rightarrow V = \bar{V} \Rightarrow M \cdot \bar{V} = P \cdot Y$$

This makes sense because in times of normal economic growth a certain amount of money supply growth is necessary to facilitate the increase in transactions. In addition, it can be shown, that a growth of the money supply in excess of this amount leads to rising inflation.

If it is additionally assumed that $\Delta Y/Y$ depends on growth in the factors of production, technological progress, human capital, and natural resources (because of the neutrality of money), the quantity theory predicts a one-for-one relation between changes in the money growth rate and changes in the inflation rate (Mankiw, Taylor 2006, p. 617). Figure no. 3 illustrates this correlation with data available from the Federal Reserve Bank of St. Louis (USA) for the United States from 1960 until 2016. The plotted moving average for the consumer price index (CPI) and $M2$ is based on the assumption, that there is a general investment cycle of an average of 8 years (based on the Juglar cycle). The delayed effect of monetary and fiscal policy measures is taken into account by about 18 months, based on assumptions by Milton Friedman (Wildmann 2012, p. 87; Socher 1971, p. 66). The following formula was used for the moving average:

$m_{n,t}$ = simple moving average of M2 and CPI

n = 96 months and 114 months

x = M2 and CPI

t = date

$$m_{n,t} = \frac{1}{n} \sum_{i=0}^{n-1} x_{(t-i)} \qquad (2.2.3)$$

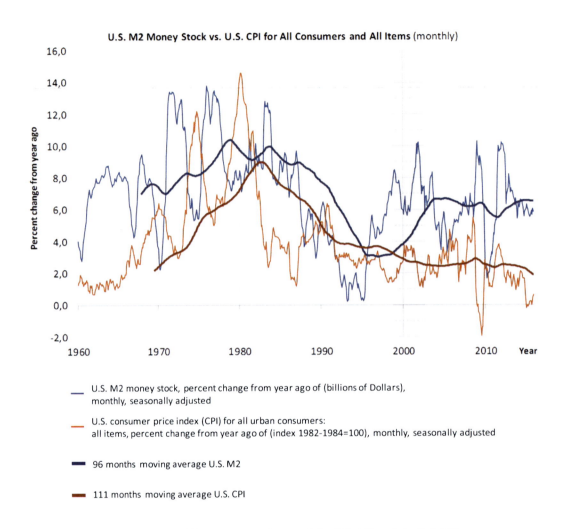

Figure 3: Monthly percentage change of the U.S. M2 and the U.S. CPI
with corresponding moving average
(Illustration by author, data source: Federal Reserve Bank of St. Louis 2016b)

In the long-run it seems, that inflation and money growth follow the same trends, at least in the USA. However, there is an interesting and distinctive deviation from the long-run trend in the diagram during the recession phase between 1999 and 2003.

New Classical Macroeconomics Theory of Inflation[8]

New classical macroeconomics is based on monetarism and implies essentially rational expectations of economic agents (Anderegg 2007, p. 215). This theory assumes full price flexibility, and that the market clears at all times, which means that at any one time the economy is able to establish a unique equilibrium at full employment, or the highest level of real GDP through price and wage adjustment. Moreover, the quantity equation is valid, as well as the neutrality of money. Inflation is only caused through money supply increases that surpass the changing demand for transaction balances, monetary shocks, such as unanticipated money supply changes, and real shocks, that unfold pricing effects (ibid.). A policy change must therefore come as a surprise to the people and discretionary changes in policy must be avoided (Dwivedi 2010, pp. 371 ff.). These policy implications can be considered as a stark contrast to the Keynesian and monetarist policy prescriptions. Nevertheless, the micro foundations on the assumption of rationally acting agents have been included in the New Keynesian economics as well. In addition, the new classical macroeconomics model has also established the concept of expected inflation within rational expectations (Arnold 2008, p. 265). In case of expected inflation, economic agents are prepared that year after year the prices as well as income increase by the level of expected inflation. In general inflation expectations for a certain period are a conception that an economic agent evolves about inflation before that period.

Costs of Inflation

Among scholars prevails the opinion, that a certain amount of inflation is better than deflation (Mehta 2000, p. 95). The reason is mainly the general fear, that if people think prices for goods will decrease in the future, they could postpone consumption. Such a situation can cause a downward spiral, where people buy less and less. This also applies to companies (Kenneth 1950, pp. 62 ff.; Mehta 2000, p. 95). Moreover, in such a condition, the falling prices will lower profit margins of companies. This is empirical verifiable and its most famous example is Japan, where deflation started in the early 1990s and was accompanied by a deep

---

[8] There is a debate going on today between New Keynesians and new classical macroeconomists and it seems that the support of the new classical model is increasing (Dwivedi 2010, p. 372). Nowadays, there is consensus that the hypothesis of the ineffectiveness of monetary policy is represented only barely.

recession and a rise in unemployment. Therefore, an inflation rate in the low single-digits can avoid deflationary tendencies and creates leeway for companies to increase wages. The classical theory and its concept of the neutrality of money states additionally, that a change in the price level is merely a change in the units of measurement. This is inter alia the reason why inflation does not reduce real wages, because in the long-run, real wage is only determined by labor supply and the marginal product of labor. Only in the short-run, when nominal wages are fixed by contracts, inflation has a real impact on purchasing power. However, based on the concept of money illusion, the quantity theory of money assumes that people belief that changes in nominal wages/prices represent changes in real wages/prices. In such a case the nominal value of money is mistaken for its purchasing power. Nevertheless, the money illusion is a prerequisite for the effectiveness of monetary policy measures (Jain, Khanna 2011, p. 519). Accordingly, while low inflation can be considered as a good condition, there are several costs which arise from inflation, mainly adjustment costs. Economists have identified six costs of inflation, where it plays an important role, whether inflation was anticipated by economic agents or not (Mankiw 2015, pp. 358 ff.).

- **Shoe leather costs** (expected inflation costs)
  Costs that incur by the disadvantage of lower cash holdings.

- **Menu costs** (expected inflation costs)
  Costs that occur when prices have to be adjusted.

- **Relative price variability** (expected inflation costs)
  Costs that incur when prices may become outdated.

- **Tax distortions** (expected inflation costs)
  Unfair tax treatment that occur if tax liabilities change due to nonindexation of the tax code, e.g. capital gain taxes even if inflation was anticipated.

- **Confusion and inconvenience** (expected inflation costs)
  Costs that incur from a changing unit of account, difficult comparison of nominal values and long-range financial planning.

- **Arbitrary redistribution of wealth** (unexpected inflation costs)
  Costs that occur when the actual inflation rate turns out to be different from the expected inflation rate.

Mankiw (2015) also notes, that during hyperinflation (inflation > 50%) many of these costs are large, but it is also less clear how large these costs are when there is only moderate inflation (Mankiw 2015, p. 358).

Measurement of Inflation

The measurement of inflation is generally based on price indices. In case of the inflation rate, of which is generally spoken about, the consumer price index (CPI) measures the average price development of goods and services that households buy for consumption purposes. This includes, for example, food, clothing and motor vehicles as well as rent, cleaning services or repairs (Federal Statistical Office of Germany 2016a). This so-called basket of goods is a representative of a typical household of an economic region. Other typical and important indices are the producer price index (PPI), the import price index (IPI), the export price index (XPI), and the price index of the gross domestic product, or short GDP deflator (Kampmann, Walter 2013, p. 16). In Europe, each country calculates its own national CPI. Thus, there are different national criteria, composition and weightings in the index formation of each country. In Germany, the national CPI consists of about 600 types of goods and circa 300,000 individual prices (Federal Statistical Office of Germany 2016a). Quantitative and qualitative changes of products are also considered in calculation of the index. Decreases a supplier the packaging size of a product at a constant price, it is treated as a price increase in the price statistics. To establish comparability of indices between countries of the euro area, the national CPI is adjusted methodologically and a harmonized index of consumer prices (HICP) is calculated by each country. Each national statistical office reports Eurostat the appropriate data and Eurostat subsequently calculates the HICP for the euro area as a whole. The basis for the calculation constitutes the Council Regulation (EC) No. 2494/95 from October 23rd 1995 about harmonized indices of consumer prices (Federal Statistical Office of Germany 2016b).[9] Regarding the calculating of an overall consumer price index for the euro area, the weighting of the country depends on its contribution to the total consumption expenditure. The following illustration provides an overview of the weights of the main product groups in the HICP for the euro area as a whole.

---

[9] The previous year comparison of a CPI shows accelerated price increases from month to month delayed, which means that the consumer price index is a lagging indicator. At this point, producer price indices give usually price information in better time (Kampmann, Walter 2013, p. 15).

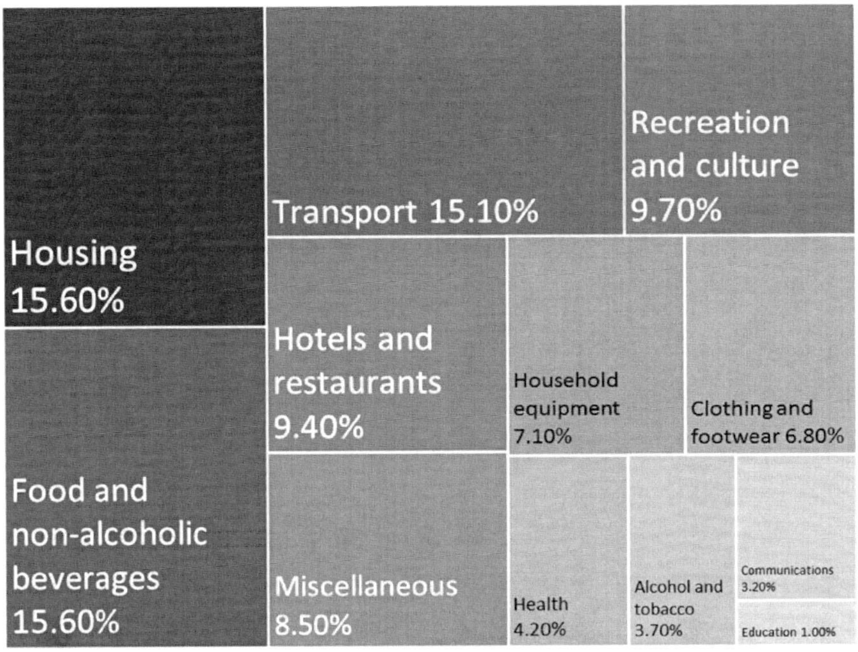

15.60% Housing
(rent, electricity, gas, etc.)

15.60% Food and non-alcoholic beverages
(bread and cereals, vegetables, etc.)

15.10% Transport
(cars, petrol, train tickets, etc.)

9.70% Recreation and culture
(digital cameras, cinema tickets, etc.)

9.40% Hotels and restaurants
(restaurants and cafés, etc.)

8.50% Miscellaneous
(hairdressers, house insurance, etc.)

7.10% Household equipment
(carpets, household appliances, etc.)

6.80% Clothing and footwear
(clothing, shoe repair, etc.)

4.20% Health
(medicines, dental services, etc.)

3.70% Alcohol and tobacco
(wine, beer, cigarettes, etc.)

3.20% Communications
(telephone bills, stamps, etc.)

1.00% Education
(school fees, language courses, etc.)

Figure 4: Weights of the main product groups in the euro area HICP
(Illustration by author, data source: ECB 2016c)

The calculation of the indices is usually done by two methods: calculation according Laspeyers and according Paasche (Wildmann 2012, p. 54). A Paasche price index calculates the price increase by the weighting of the prices of different periods by the quantity of the current period. This index examines what a current basket of goods costs and what for the same basket in the base year would have had been paid. The GDP deflator is an example of a Paasche price index.

With i = good/asset, 0 = base year, t = reporting year, p = price, q = quantity, the Paasche price index can be expressed as follows (Blanchard, Illing 2009, p. 81):

p_i^t = prices regarding the reporting year
p_i^0 = prices regarding the base year
q_i^t = consumption regarding reporting year

$$CPI_{PA} = \frac{\sum_{i=1}^{n} p_i^t \cdot q_i^t}{\sum_{i=1}^{n} p_i^0 \cdot q_i^t} = \frac{\sum_{i=1}^{n} \frac{p_i^t}{p_i^0} \cdot p_i^0 \cdot q_i^t}{\sum_{i=1}^{n} p_i^0 \cdot q_i^t} \quad (2.2.4)$$

A Laspeyres price index, on the other hand weights prices each with the quantities of the base period. This index examines what the basket of goods would cost in the reporting period and what have had to be paid for the same basket in the base year. As consumers try to substitute expensive goods with cheaper, the Laspeyres index usually oversubscribes inflation (ibid.). With the same index of letters and values as from the Paasche price index, a Laspeyres price index can be expressed as follows (Wildmann 2012, p. 54):

p_i^t = prices regarding the reporting year
p_i^0 = prices regarding the base year
q_i^0 = consumption regarding the base year

$$CPI_{LA} = \frac{\sum_{i=1}^{n} p_i^t \cdot q_i^0}{\sum_{i=1}^{n} p_i^0 \cdot q_i^0} = \frac{\sum_{i=1}^{n} \frac{p_i^t}{p_i^0} \cdot p_i^0 \cdot q_i^0}{\sum_{i=1}^{n} p_i^0 \cdot q_i^0} \quad (2.2.5)$$

The HICP in Germany is also calculated on the basis of a Laspeyres price index. There are some important aspects which are worth mentioning. The HICP of Germany is calculated by the following equation, where p = prices, q = quantities, and j = goods of the coverage (Elbel, Preißmann 2012, pp. 672 ff.):

$$HVPI_t(2015) = \sum_j \frac{p_{j,t(2015)}}{p_{j,Dec2014}} \times \frac{(p_{j,Dec2014} \cdot q_{j,2013})}{\sum_j (p_{j,Dec2014} \cdot q_{j,2013})} \quad (2.2.6)$$

The formula above is a chain link of the entire price index and is only valid for the corresponding period, in this case from January 2015 until December 2015. The first fraction of the formula represents the price measurement numbers and the expressions in brackets of the right side of the formula can be determined by using the following substitution:

$$\left(p_{j,Dec2014} \cdot q_{j,2013}\right) = \left(p_{j,2010} \cdot q_{j,2010}\right) \cdot \frac{p_{j,2013} \cdot q_{j,2013}}{p_{j,2010} \cdot q_{j,2010}} \cdot \frac{p_{j,Dec2014}}{p_{j,2013}}$$

A new component of the formula is the fraction in the middle of the equation above. Here, the average annual expenditures from 2013 (the year before the last year) are put into relation with the corresponding amounts of expenditure in 2010. Weighting base and index base are therefore 2010 and price base is December of the previous year, so December 2014. The choice of the type of index and its method will cause significantly different outcomes. However, the most commonly used methods result in similar findings (Miles et al. 2014, p. 343). The inflation rate is finally calculated by comparing the price of the basket of goods (value of the CPI) of a given month with the price of the same month of the previous year. The inflation rate thus corresponds to the percentage change of the CPI over a certain period of time. Inflation rate can be calculated on a monthly basis as well as on a yearly basis. Typically, however, the inflation rate is usually calculated on a yearly basis (Wildman 2012, p. 54).

Development of Inflation

The following illustration compares the development of inflation of the euro area (19 countries), USA, and Japan, three of the world's strongest economic regions.

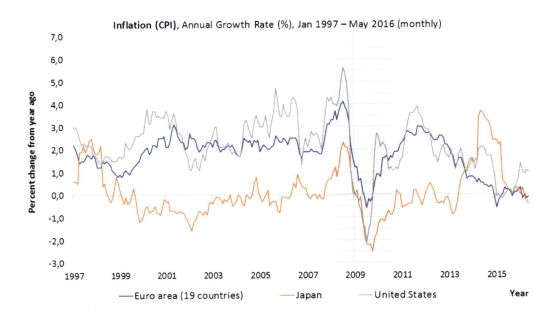

Figure 5: Development of inflation of the euro area, Japan, and USA, based on a monthly basis (Illustration by author, data source: OECD 2016a)

It is empirically verifiable, that global events, particularly changes in oil prices have led to inflation of similar development within industrial nations. But already small differences in inflation rates may lead over time to significant differences in price levels of different countries (Miles et al. 2014, p. 340). Figure 5 also shows the impact of the latest global financial crisis (shaded gray in the figure).

2.3. Interest Rates

Another important component within the theory of money are interest rates. According to the German Federal Bank (2016), an interest is generally the price of the temporarily and loan based allocation of money, respectively capital, which the borrower or capital seeker pays the investor or capital provider. The ratio is usually expressed as a percentage per annum. Typically, the interest rate is higher, the longer a loan runs. Other determinants of the amount of interest, for example, are the estimated risk of default of a loan and the quality of a possible collateral. The interest level in turn gives information about the average height of interest rates for a specified term on a specific market (Deutsche Bundesbank 2016b).

Theoretical Explanation of Interest

Within the scope of science, there are different approaches to explain and describe the nature of interest. As with the theoretical analysis and description of the nature of money, there are also different schools of thoughts that deal with the subject of interest rates. It is useful to give a brief overview of the main theories and categories before continuing with a further list and description of different types of interest. According to Stoerrle (1970), it is institutionally differentiated between the following types, respectively categories of interest theories (Stoerrle 1970, p. 42):

- Interest theories in a static or stationary economy.
- Interest theories in a dynamic or progressive economy.

Nowadays, a thematic discussion of money and interest with respect to its functions and effectiveness within the monetary and financial system is considerably important, not least because of the recent financial crisis, which has shaken several economic dogmas. The most recognized functional subdivision of interest theories is as follows (ibid.):

- Real interest theory.
- Monetary interest theory.

The **real interest theory** explains the interest as the price, which brings savings and investments into balance. In this case, the level of an interest rate is determined by the savings. The more is saved, the lower the interest rate and the higher the investment incentives. In such a case, the demand of capital for investment purposes goes beyond the amount of savings. Thus, the interest rate will increase until so much capital demand is eliminated, that there is an equilibrium again. This means, that the amount of investments can never be larger than the savings and the interest regulates (Panten et al. 1975, p. 233). Another explanation was brought forward from Boehm-Bawerk (1921). He describes the interest as an incentive for the lender to shift his consumption hypothetically into the future (Müller 2015, pp 163 ff.).

The **monetary interest theory** on the other hand considers the interest as the price to give up liquidity. This theory implies that economic agents have a propensity for assets in the most liquid form. According to this, the interest is a cost factor, which provides a compensation for the loss, which represents the illiquidity compared to liquidity. The monetary interest theory also argues that the interest is independent of savings and thus no function of the volume of savings. The level of interest rates is only determined by the earnings prospects of a planned investment, compared to more liquid forms of money investments. In this context, it is important to be aware of the assumptions made by the theory that money represents the highest degree of freedom of choice for economic agents. Money that can be issued within the shortest possible time to buy goods, represents this freedom of choice most unambiguously (Panten et al. 1975, p. 233). This is the reason why short-term investments have the lowest interest. The most important and most famous representatives of this theory are Gesell and Keynes. The liquidity preference is particularly acknowledged in the liquidity preference theory of Keynes (Mueller 2015, pp. 562 ff.). It is also useful to mention here the importance of the IS-LM model for the monetary interest theory. It refers to a model, which describes the macroeconomic balance by taking into account the real sector (goods market) and monetary sector (money market).[10]

---

[10] The IS-LM model has been heavily criticized and modified in recent years, because some important aspects of the model are partly no longer compatible with real observations (Bofinger 2015, pp. 495 ff.).

The theoretical explanation of interest is one of the most difficult areas within the science of national economy (Panten et al. 1975, p. 233). The real interest theory refers to savings and investment, the monetary interest theory to money supply and liquidity preference. Therefore, it should be noted, that each of the two theoretical models of explanation has certain biases. It is important during evaluation and gaining knowledge to merge both theories and check assumptions for plausibility.

Types of Interest Rates

Within the framework of national accounting, capital is usually categorized between money capital, physical capital, and human capital (Stobbe 1994, p. 438). The following table shows the corresponding types of interest.

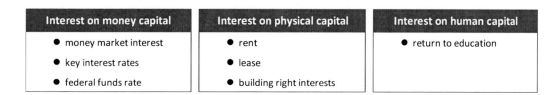

Table 3: Classification of interest rates based on capital forms
(Illustration by author, data source: Stobbe 1994 p. 438, Harmon et al. 2000)

Another possibility to classify types of interest is based on the criteria where interest rates occur and who is the issuer. According to Duwendag (1999) one group of interest rates are **central bank interest rates**. These interest rates are set by the central bank. The monetary policy activity of a central bank is manifested in the variation of these interest rates. Central bank interest rates relate generally to loans receivable of the central bank to commercial banks and are therefore an integral part of the supply of central bank money (Duwendag et al. 1999, pp. 63 ff.). Every central bank of an industrial developed state issues such interest rates, for example the interest rate for main refinancing operations (MRO) of the ECB, the primary credit rate of the FED, or the basic loan rate of the BOJ. Short-term interest rates are an important part of the money market and are also called **money market interest rates**. The money market is a market on which banks can compensate different liquidity facilities. This is usually done by banks with current cash surpluses that borrow cash resources to banks with current liquidity needs in the form of a money market loan. Supply and demand usually set the money market interest rates for these money market loans or reference rates provide a range. A very important interest rate on the money market is the overnight rate, which is an interest rate on loans over one day. However, different forms of overnight transactions can be described as overnight loan, but they are all bound to a specific interest rate (Duwendag et al. 1999, p. 64). Long-term interest rates are the counterpart of short-term interest rates and as **capital market interest rates** they are part of the capital market. This is mainly about interest rates on long-term financing. A typical example are fixed income securities, which are issued for long-term funding. Representative for the capital market is the yield on bonds outstanding, so the interest of already circulating securities. The yield on bonds outstanding in Germany, for example, is determined by the Central bank of Germany. These yields are published grouped by issuer (public authorities, banks, etc.) and maturities (Duwendag et al. 1999, p. 65). For the average consumer, like the customer of commercial banks, classic **debit and credit interest rates** play an important role. Debit interest rates are the interest rates that commercial banks charge their customers for loans substantially. Credit interest rates are the interest rates customers receive for their deposits from commercial banks (Duwendag et al. 1999, p. 65). The following list provides an overview of selected interest rates within the euro area.

Interest rate	Maturity	Creditor	Debitor
Central bank interest rates			
Interest rate for *main refinancing operations* of the ECB	short-time	CB	ComB
Interest rate for *marginal lending facility* of the ECB	short-time	CB	ComB
Deposit facility rate of the ECB	short-time	ComB	CB
Money market interest rates			
Overnight rate (interbank rate)	short-time	ComB	ComB
European Interbank Offered Rate (EURIBOR)	short-time	ComB	ComB
London Interbank Offered Rate (LIBOR)	short-time	ComB	ComB
Capital market interest rates			
Yield on bonds outstanding	long/short-time	ComB, PH, CB[11]	ComB, Corp, PA
Interest rates on fixed income securities	long-time	ComB, PH, CB[11]	ComB, Corp, PA
Debit and credit interest rates			
Overdraft facility interest rate	long-time	ComB	PH, Corp
Savings deposits interest rate	long/short-time	ComB	PH, Corp

CB: Central Bank
ComB: Commercial Bank
Corp: Corporation, Production Company
PH: Private Households
PA: Public Authorities

Table 4: Overview of selected interest rates within the euro area
(Illustration by author, data source: Duwendag et al. 1999, p. 64)[11]

---

[11] Since 2010, the ECB buys within its easing of monetary policy government bonds, and since 2016 also corporate bonds and is therefore also a creditor (Hedtstück 2016).

2.4. Monetary Policy

Money and interest rates are by far the most important variables within the monetary theory. As seen in chapter 2.1, the currency that is established as money in developed societies has no intrinsic value. As a result, its value and the amount can be influenced by the issuing institutions to gain general acceptance and trust among trading partners as well as the general public for this kind of money. The question, which arises in this context is the following: How and by whom are the variables money and interest controlled to implement strategic and political objectives?

According to Dwivedi (2010) *"Monetary policy, in general, refers to the action undertaken by the monetary authorities to control and regulate the demand for and the supply of money with a given purpose."* (Dwivedi 2010, p. 577). Such a purpose usually includes objectives as monetary stability, growth promotion, and promotion of employment. These objectives of monetary policy can be achieved either through shortage of the money supply (more expensive loans with higher interest rates, restrictive monetary policy) or through expansion of the money supply (cheapening of credit by low interest rates, expansionary monetary policy) (European Parliament 2016a). Monetary policy can be considered as a powerful tool of economic control and management of the economy along with fiscal policy. Fiscal policy, on the other hand, includes all political measures, for example by legislation, that affect the state budget by income and/or expenditure. The main measures are the determination of taxes and subsidies, borrowing and the adoption of the budget. In addition to a regulation of income and expenditure by the state, fiscal policy can also pursue broader objectives like promoting social justice or influencing business activity, respectively economic cycles (ibid.). The main theoretical frameworks for monetary policy nowadays are also monetarism and Keynesianism (Arnold 2008, pp. 335 ff.).

While classical economics considers money as neutral without an impact on real economy, **Keynesian economics** expects real economic consequences of monetary policy. By Keynesian perception, the interest rate is the most important determinant for investment activities and monetary policy is therefore considered in terms of interest rate policy (Anderegg 2007, p. 112). Keynes point of view contrasted with the classical view, that money supply only controls prices. He argued that a restrictive monetary policy could also risk a decrease of price levels and a decline of wages and thereby trigger a deflationary depression (Anderegg

2007, p. 181). The post-Keynesian doctrine stresses the importance of countercyclical monetary policy to compensate fluctuations in the money supply, which are caused by a cyclical credit creation by banks during boom and contraction periods (Anderegg 2007, p. 290).

From a **monetarist point of view**, money supply policy plays a central role. Monetarists argue for predictable and consistent conditions for the economy, rather than for short-term interventions. The central objective is price stability. To ensure this, they recommend a rules-based monetary growth. The monetary theory of one of the greatest proponent of monetarism, Milton Friedman, cannot be refuted as a matter of principle even today. A to expansionary monetary policy is still the cause for the emergence of inflation, respectively higher price levels. This was even the case during the quantitative easing (QE) program by the FED from 2009-2013, and the QE program by the BOJ from 2013-2015, although the expected impact partly failed to meet its forecasts (author's note: see development of inflation in figure 5). Monetary growth and inflation are therefore connected to each other in the long-term perspective. The forecast of inflation, is difficult because of price shocks, which complicate the prediction of the effect of monetary policy (Anderegg 2007, p. 300).

Objectives of Monetary Policy

In countries where a rather Keynesian policy is pursued, the central bank has mainly growth and employment objectives. In countries with a more monetarist economic policy, the focus is more on price stability. Nevertheless, such a distinction is difficult and not always easily possible. According to Ruckriegel et al. (2006) and the Gabler economic lexicon (2016a), monetary policy is usually distinguished between operational objectives, intermediate objectives, and ultimate objectives of monetary policy, and sometimes separately direct inflation targeting (Gabler Economic Lexicon 2016a; Ruckriegel et al. 2006, p. 698).

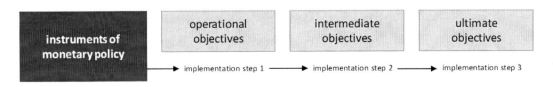

Figure 6: General objectives of monetary policy
(Illustration by author, data source: Ruckriegel et al. 2006, p. 698)

Operational objectives of monetary policy can be considered as economic variables, which a central bank can control by using its instruments. At the instrument level, the central bank sets key interest rates in order to achieve firstly their operational objective. Short-term money market interest rates, e.g. the interbank rate, are one other main operational objective. In Europe, the interbank rate is geared to the marginal lending facility rate of the ECB. This rate can be controlled and regulated daily within the framework of the central bank's liquidity management (ibid.). Its counterpart in the U.S. is the Federal funds rate which is used by banks among themselves to borrow money. The primary credit rate that is issued by the FED applies to loans extended by the FED to banks for a short duration, usually overnight (Madura 2014, p. 727). In Japan, the counterparts are the basic discount rates and basic loan rates (Bank of Japan 2016a). Alternatively, a lot-size, like the monetary base can also be used. In this case the central bank tries to manage the currency in circulation, plus reserve holdings. Because banks can influence the monetary base via their deposit structure or their refinancing behavior, the monetary base is often corrected (Gabler Economic Lexicon 2016a).

Intermediate objectives of monetary policy are ideally good and short-term observable and are simultaneously in a sufficiently close relationship to the economic objective (ibid.). Common intermediate objectives are the money supply, interest rates, inflation itself, and sometimes currency rates. Nowadays intermediate objectives have lost somewhat of importance in practical monetary policy. However, the distinction between the operational and intermediate level makes clear, that a non-consideration of money on the operational level is not necessarily equivalent to a non-observance of monetary developments in general (Ruckriegel et al. 2006, p. 699). Unless nowadays central banks do not omit intermediate objectives completely, they are often interpreted as indicator variables (Gabler Economic Lexicon 2016a). If the money supply is controlled as an intermediate objective, the procedure is based on the assumption of monetarism, that the demand for money is stable in the long-term in an economy. With the rule for monetary growth, which can be derived from the quantity equation of money, it is possible to stimulate economic growth while on the other hand no inflation comes up.[12] During liquidity management as an intermediate objective, the lending process and the associated credit costs are taken into focus. Credit supply and credit demand are regulated by the central bank through control of the free liquidity reserves and by using the interest rate policy (ibid.). The influencing of currency rates is especially useful for small countries with a large foreign trade. The local currency is unilaterally pegged at a fixed exchange rate to a foreign currency (lead currency) or to a basket of foreign currencies (currency board) (Schmolke et al. 2016, p. 11). One goal is to import a higher reputation and confidence from a foreign central bank. Some countries turn away from monetary strategies that include explicit intermediate targets. Instead central banks base their monetary policy directly on inflation within the scope of inflation targeting. In this case, policymakers set an inflation target and observe the current price level increase as well as leading indicators for future price developments. Central banks adjust their monetary policy interventions on the expected inflation potential in this context. Direct inflation targeting has strongly gained in importance in opposition to a monetary supply targeting since the 1990s. The large North American central banks (Federal Reserve, Bank of Canada), as well as the Reserve Bank of Australia, the Reserve Bank of New Zealand, and now the ECB pursue a monetary policy strategy in recent years, which is aligned with a direct inflation targeting (Gabler Economic Lexicon 2016a).

Ultimate objectives are objectives that a central bank wants to achieve in the medium or long-term. Until recently it was believed that central banks should only focus on combating inflation and maintaining price stability, but since the last global financial crisis, economic dogmas and views have changed (Ruckriegel et al. 2006, p. 699). Today there is an academic discussion going on about the central bank's mandate (Georgsson et al. 2015, Abstract). The need to lend money to payment system participants during a crisis without increasing the risk of moral hazard are currently subjects of discussion as well as the possibility to extend central bank tasks beyond their fundamental activities, and in particular the responsibility for macro-prudential policy and supervision of banks and other financial institutions

---

[12] In doing so, the growth of the money supply must correlate with the sum of the growth of the real domestic product and the acceptable or inevitable price level increase, reduced by the trend correlated change in the velocity of money (Ruckriegel et al. 2006, p. 699).

(ibid.). An important conclusion from the recent financial crisis is the need of financial stability that has become an important goal for authorities, which is debated whether to include it on the objectives list of central banks or authorize another institution to achieve it (Badea 2015, Abstract). Nevertheless, the ultimate goal of a central bank is usually specified by the statutes of legislature (Ruckriegel et al. 2006, p. 700).

Discretionary versus Rule-based Monetary Policy

From a strategic perspective, monetary policy can be distinguished situational. In case of a discretionary monetary policy, monetary policy decision makers decide for each case what kind of policy measures they will use to achieve their objective. Monetary policy is therefore in relation to the characteristics of the problem situation and hence may not be consistent over time. The advantage of a discretionary strategy is the flexibility to maneuver. However, a disadvantage can result if this form of policy is unpredictable from the perspective of market participants and thereby create expectation uncertainty (Gabler Economic Lexicon 2016a).

In a rule-based monetary policy or open-loop policy on the other hand, the central bank is obliged to perform a certain action usually without regard to the specifics of the situation. The actions of a central bank are determined accurately in this case and the central bank has no discretionary leeway. The commitment to increase the monetary base annually by a constant rate, would be an example of such a rigid rule. A major advantage of this strategy is the reliability of expectations from market participants that can anticipate the changes in the monetary base and thus are able to take this into account within their individual economic plans. Finally, this strategy may result in a higher credibility of monetary policy, which ensures confidence in the functioning of the monetary system. However, there is still the disadvantage that a central bank cannot respond differentiated to different inflation or deflation causes. Also, a rule-based strategy is a strategy, where action rules are triggered during the occurrence of specific events. In this case, a feedback exists between target and the choice or use of the instrument. This so called closed-loop-policy also ensures stability of expectations for monetary policy. At the same time, such a rule binding is relatively flexible to different situations and causes of inflation or deflation. This applies of course only to the extent that all relevant positional parameters are detected. Therefore, this rule-based strategy remains still inflexible towards unexpected causes of undesirable developments. Therefore, it is unavoidable, to keep leeway to monetary policy actors (ibid.).

Expansionary monetary policy

Monetary policy is differentiated primarily between two variants: expansive and restrictive monetary policy. Expansionary monetary policy is a policy to expand money supply mainly by keeping interest rates low (Wiley 2015, p. 39). To achieve this objective of monetary policy, several monetary policy instruments are available to the central bank, for example open market operations, the offering of standing facilities, and the requirement of deposit reserves from commercial banks. But expansionary monetary policy is also reflected by the central bank in the form of purchases of certain securities and bills of exchange. In the context of open market operations, the central bank can purchase securities and bonds on the securities market. An expansionary monetary policy pursues the lowering of reserve requirements and thus enables the emergence of excess reserves. This policy mainly seeks to encourage private lending by companies, individuals and banks (OpenStax College 2014, p. 569). In the short-term, expansionary monetary policy lowers interest rates and at the same time increases production and price levels. The purchase of assets from banks, also called quantitative easing (QE), has the effect of lowering yields on bonds and creating cheaper borrowing conditions for banks. This in turn has the consequence that banks' capacity to lend to individuals and businesses increases (Financial Times 2016). The theoretical approach to explain these mechanisms of action is based on a Keynesian view by using the famous IS–LM model, resp. AD–AS model (Sawyer, Sprinkle 2015, pp. 514 ff.). In the long-run, a nominal increase in the money supply affects neither production nor interest rates but only the price levels. This is because additional production lowers unemployment and hence wages rise and later prices follow. Here, the already addressed neutrality of money in the previous chapters plays the decisive role in the medium term. As the theoretical approach to describe the effects of an expansion of the money supply on inflation, the quantity equation from the quantity theory of money is used. Worth mentioning in the context of an expansionary monetary policy is that *"economists of the rational expectations school believe that if the economy is already producing its potential, an expansionary policy, if fully anticipated, has no effect on output or employment, not even in the short-run."* (McEachern 2015, p. 264).

Expansionary monetary policy usually entails a depreciation of the domestic currency. The downward pressure on the currency exchange rate is caused by capital outflows to higher-yield markets, because of lower interest rates in the domestic market. In a system with flexible currency exchange rates, which is the case for almost every country in the western hemisphere, capital flows are mostly responsive to interest rate differentials. Furthermore, in the medium-term the depreciation of the currency will also increase net exports and reinforce the aggregate demand impact on investment and consumption spending (Wiley 2015, p. 39). In the long-run capital outflow causes a shortage of money supply and thereby increasing interest rates. Thus, the effects generated by the central bank may partly cancel each other out. This issue has gained in importance within the past decade regarding the alignment of a countries' monetary policy, especially within the global context.

Contractionary monetary policy

A contractionary monetary policy essentially includes any measure, which reduces the supply of money (OpenStax College 2014, p. 578). In addition to conventional monetary policy instruments, the central bank may also use open market operations to reduce the monetary base. This is typically done through the sale of securities for cash. Another way to reduce the money supply and taking money out of circulation is raising the bond rate to encourage long-term borrowing. Through the removal of cash in circulation, the central bank withdraws money for the economy and thus reduces the monetary basis for the economy. Although the central bank can raise bank reserve requirements, almost no central bank of a major economy nowadays makes significant use of money aggregates to guide their policy in the short-run (McEachern 2015, p. 253). Especially in times of a cyclical overheating of the economy, a contractionary monetary policy is an effective tool that leads to lower interest rates, decline in production, and contains the risk of increased inflation. As theoretical approach to describe the effects of a contractionary monetary policy the IS–LM model, resp. AD–AS model is used regarding an expansionary monetary policy (Sawyer, Sprinkle 2015, pp. 514 ff.). In this model, it is assumed that a nominal reduction in money causes a direct reduction in money in the short-term, because the price level remains constant for the time being. Due to the decrease in the money supply and a decline in overall demand for goods, production and the price level decrease subsequently. The production decline entails now a reduction of employment, which also leads to changed price expectations. After wages have been adjusted downwards, the total offer has been adjusted again, the level of production finally will revert to a balanced state. In the medium-term, production will thus return through price adjustments to a natural level, but at a lower price level (ibid.).

Within the framework of a contractionary monetary policy, currency exchange rates play also an important role. The effects and processes in this case are inverse to an expansionary monetary policy. An increase of domestic interest rates accordingly causes an increase of the exchange rate, because foreign money flows in various domestic types of investments. In consequence, a relative increase in the prices of domestic goods compared to foreign goods occurs. Subsequently, the demand for domestic goods falls, production is falling. In turn this decline conditions a decrease in the demand for money, which leads to a decline in interest rates. Thus, the effects may partly cancel each other out as well as in the medium and long-run of an expansionary monetary policy (Wiley 2015, pp. 38 ff.).

Problem cases
The processes described above regarding the functionality of an expansive or contractive monetary policy partially based on theoretical considerations, but also empirical findings. But there are also empirical findings and theoretical considerations in which the functionality is not given any more.

A common problem case in this context is a so-called cash trap. A **cash trap** is a phenomenon during expansionary monetary policy, that occurs after a very strong economic downturn, which goes along with high overcapacity. Entrepreneurs relinquish an expansion of investments and undertake only replacement investments. Such a wait-and-see state has the consequence that a decline of interest rates does not lead to an increase of investments (Bofinger 2015, p. 409).

Another problem during expansionary monetary policy is the **liquidity trap**. Such a situation was already described by Keynes and can occur when economic agents expect no positive return on various asset classes within the economic environment of very low interest rates. Economic agents then hold additional central bank money in cash and restructure their asset positions in favor of holding money.

Investors have no longer incentives for long term investments. Consequently, a monetary expansion would not lead to an increase in overall economic activity. Keynesian-oriented economic historians are convinced that the economies of the U.S. and Britain were in a liquidity trap in the 1930s (Gabler Economic Lexicon 2016a; Anderegg 2007, p. 114). The monetarist counterpart to the liquidity trap is Friedman's money trap. Such a situation would occur if the central bank had increased the money supply significantly beyond the fixed target, so that it is reckoned by the public in general with rising prices. The financial markets then respond to the expected rise in inflation with higher nominal interest rates, which means that the expected price increase would be reflected directly in interest rate increases. An expansionary monetary policy in this case can appear even restrictive. Under these conditions, the central bank cannot set easing signals (Hennies 2005, p. 26).

Another problem, that is more of technical and organizational nature are **time delays**. The effects between changes in interest rates and induced capital goods expenditures are not immediately. Depending on maturities or the duration of investment projects, effects of changes in interest rates can only be expected with more or less long time delays (ibid.).

Another issue, that not necessarily has to be considered as a problem but as an important circumstance that may cause a lot of uncertainty, is the increase of globalization and interdependence of international financial markets. This fact has become increasingly significant after the last financial crisis. Ironically, the global interdependences of international markets and their feedback on domestic monetary policy was recognized in March 2007 already a few months before the outbreak of the crisis by Ben Bernanke, at that time head of the FED, who addressed the issue in a speech at the Stanford Institute for Economic Policy Research (Bernanke 2007). In this speech, he addressed the question whether globalization may hinder monetary policy and the ability of the FED to affect U.S. interest rates and asset prices (ibid.). Moreover, the question arises in general as to what extent the condition of a foreign economy, which is closely connected by trade relations to a domestic economy may affect the national economic policy and effectiveness of its instruments.

Beyond that, it has been found that aggressive and forcing statements by members of a central bank may have a major impact on foreign exchange rates and securities price movements - without ever walk the talk - but still move real variables of an economy, such as market interest rates and money creation (Monticini et al. 2011). There is evidence, that this kind of policy has led in recent times to the likelihood that monetary policy - if really put into action - may has become less effective in the wake of financial globalization (Belke Rees 2014; Stakić 2014).

2.5. Transmission Mechanism

The process through which monetary policy decisions affect the economy (output and employment) in general and the price level in particular is called transmission mechanism (ECB 2016c). This process can be further subdivided into different channels, where some effects occur very quickly, while others require more time, and some are even uncertain. Because of these time lags, it can be difficult to predict precise every single effect of monetary policy actions on economy, price levels, and even society in general (Deutsche Bundesbank 2016c). Economic literature has identified the existence of mainly four different channels, respectively mechanism through which monetary policy can influence economy and price levels: interest rate channel, exchange rate channel, asset price channel, and credit channel. (Belke, Polleit 2009, pp. 581 ff.; Mishkin 2015, pp. 672 ff.). Moreover, some institutions and scholars distinguish even the balance sheet channel, banking channel, or expectations channel. But for this study the first four mentioned plus the expectation channel are sufficient, because the additionally mentioned can be subsumed under the first mentioned since they are special cases of them.

Interest rate channel

Changes in interest rates of the central bank trigger adjustments to various stakeholders. These changes can have direct and indirect consequences on aggregate demand. Direct effects primarily refer to cost-of-capital effects. This means, that increased key interest rates during contractionary monetary policy periods, will also cause higher lending rates. Higher lending rates in turn curb demand for investments and consumer loans, and ultimately also a general demand for capital and consumer goods (Belke, Polleit 2009, pp. 581 ff.). Higher interest rates are an incentive for more household's savings which in turn will reduce their intention to buy goods and thus contribute to a reduction of aggregate demand. In the context of indirect effects, substitution effects in relation to a portfolio are a typical phenomenon. According to the portfolio theory and the concept of homo economicus, the main objective of investors is to have the best combination of investment alternatives in their portfolio. Accordingly, banks, businesses and households shift their asset positions as a consequence of interest rate changes by the central bank, which also has an impact on aggregate demand (Deutsche Bundesbank 2016c). Accordingly, within an environment of lower interest this effect is reverse.

Exchange rate channel

Generally, it can be assumed, if domestic interest rates rise, that capital flows from abroad. This has the consequence that the demand for the domestic currency increases, which in turn will result in its revaluation. Due to the appreciation of the domestic currency, exports become more expensive and imports cheaper and thus hinders upward price adjustments domestically. Restrictive monetary policy is therefore supported by the induced changes in exchange rates. The same applies to expansionary monetary policy (ibid.).

Asset price channel

Changes in key interest rates will also affect asset prices, for example bonds and stocks. It can be shown empirically that the prices of bonds are inversely related to the interest rates, so that higher key interest rates lower bond prices and vice versa (Belke, Polleit 2009, p. 587). A reduction in interest rates means that bonds look less attractive than shares. Thus, the share demand is stimulated, which in turn lets share prices rise. Higher interest rates in turn imply lower stock prices, because the expected future cash flows are discounted by a larger factor, which means that the present value of any given future income stream declines (ibid.). Another important area of influence of interest rates is the housing market. A rate cut may cause a decrease of financing costs, which means that real estate prices rise (Mishkin 2007).

Credit channel

In literature, the credit channel is usually discussed in two distinct but complementary ways. The focus can be placed on the one hand on the balance of the bank and on the other hand on the balance of a company. Thus, the transmission is differentiated at the level of lenders and at the level of the borrowers. If a bank grants a loan, it usually lends against a collateral. If, for example, the price level of a collateral rises in the course of expansionary monetary policy, banks receive capital gains with the result that their equity capital increase. Increased equity capital, in turn, allows banks to engage in more lending. In macroeconomic terms, this means that debt financed investments rise and thus output (Belke, Polleit 2009, pp. 597 ff.). On the borrowers' site, however, the financial 'health' of borrowers can affect their access to credit. In this case their financial 'health' is largely determined by changes in borrowers' asset values and cash flows because of a changed monetary policy. Thereby, a change in firms' net value may also affect adverse selection and moral hazard in lending to these firms (Belke, Pollein 2009, p. 598).

Expectation channel

According to Deutsche Bundesbank (2016), the expectations channel describes the concept, where investors consider an expected rise of inflation into the returns they expect to receive for providing borrowed capital over an extended period of time (Deutsche Bundesbank 2016c). The same applies to price settings of companies and the process of negotiating wages. They act quasi pre-emptively by aligning the expected inflation rate on experience. Note, that this all applies predominantly in the long-run (ibid.).

The following illustration provides an overview of the transmission mechanism of monetary policy, based on assumptions by the ECB. Since monetary policies slightly differ from central bank to central bank, this applies also to the used instrument. An illustration like the following would then appear slightly different regarding the respective central bank.

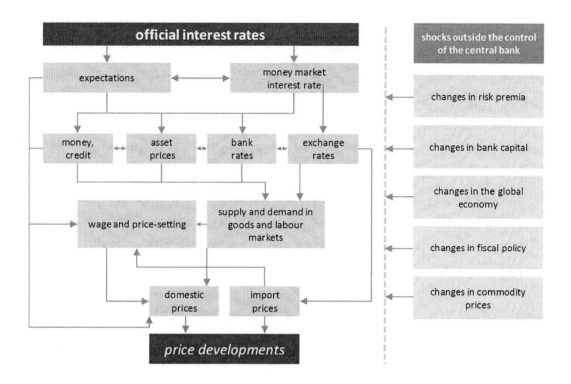

Figure 7: Main transmission channels of monetary policy decisions
(Illustration by author, data source: ECB 2016c)

2.6. Financial Repression

The issue of financial repression is politically loaded and economically ambiguous. Wrong conclusions can be easily drawn from a misunderstand of this topic, which have political and social significance. The term financial repression is often used in the context of obstructions of financial concerns in the third world through state interventions and regulations that led to the development of dual financial markets. In this case interest rates are often determined by purely administrative or political decisions and if set low enough, the financial sector will suffer because of the lack of incentives for lenders (Barrows, Smithin 2009, p. 51). In this case, financial repression has profoundly negative effects on economic growth (Montiel 2011, p. 497). Since the last economic crisis and the unconventional measures of large central banks such as the FED or the ECB, this very topic has become relevant for a description of current economic conditions in the Western world. The concept of financial repression goes back to McKinnon (1973) and Shaw (1973), who were the first to explicate the notion of financial repression. They described general government measures aimed at stabilizing markets as financial repression, which divert resources from private to state entities (Portland State University 2016). They found that many countries, even developed ones had in the past restricted competition in the financial sector with government interventions and regulations. A famous example of financial repression was observed in Mexico in the 1980s where the state took control of all banks to secure public savings (ibid.). The development strategy pursued by Chinese leadership since the latest financial crisis, which is highly reliant on investment and infrastructure projects, is also considered as financial repression among some scholars (Körner 2013, p. 108). Some scholars even assume that the financial repression and the pent-up consumption are the main reasons for lowering inflation over the past ten years in China (ibid.). The main reason for a state to implement financial repression, is its intention to take control of financial resources. By taking direct control over the financial system, the state gains access to capital without going through legislative procedures. Another objective may be to implement some kind of industrial policy. In this case, government directives for banks ensure an allocation of credit at subsidized rates for specific firms (Portland State University 2016). The economists Reinhart and Sbrancia (2011) determine financial repression by the following characteristics (Reinhart, Sbrancia, 2011, pp. 19 ff.):

- Interest rates are capped explicitly or indirectly, such as on government debt and deposit rates.
- Nationalization of banks and financial institutions with barriers that limit other institutions from entering the market.
- High reserve requirements.
- Banks are required to buy bonds of their own state or to keep as reserves.
- Imposition of capital controls, e.g. government restrictions for transfers of assets abroad.

The reason, why the topic of financial repression has become popular in the last years in Europe and the United States, is due to the great support measures by their central banks. The German Council of Economic Experts even argues that the bond purchases by the FED, Bank of England, and ECB to reduce public debt in the respective countries, can be considered as financial repression. Due to low inflation and low interest rates on government bonds (partly negative interest rates), there is a hidden reallocation of holders of government bonds in favor of the state (German Council of Economic Experts 2013, p. 84). This argumentation follows Hoffmann and Zemanek (2012), which conclude in their research study from 2012 that the FED directly represses U.S. bond yields and assists in financing the state budget, as well as the ECB conducts actions that repress interest rates, ease debt-servicing costs in all European countries and reduce the interest rate payments for the German government by about one to two per cent of total government revenues (Hoffmann, Zemanek 2012, Abstract). This research will therefore even play its part to investigate, if there are indications that underpin the aforementioned statements by examine the context of declining yield levels in comparison to the real interest rate.

3. The European Central Bank

Control of the money supply and the general implementation of economic policies is the responsibility of central banks. Decisions on monetary policy in Germany and in the member states of the European monetary union shall adopt the ECB. In the following, the ECB is presented in more detail. First, their historical development is examined, followed by an explanation of its principles, objectives and instruments.

3.1. History and Structure

The path towards the foundation of the ECB took place over several years and ran across the European Economic Community (EEC) and the subsequent joint Economic and Monetary Union (EMU). It is generally accepted, that the year 1958 could be seen as a possible starting point, the year in which the Treaties of Rome were negotiated (Scheller 2004, p. 15).

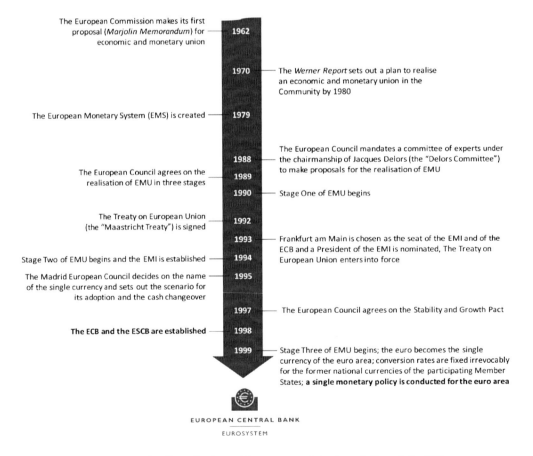

Figure 8: Timeline of selected key events of the foundation of the ECB
(Illustration by author, data source: Scheller 2004, pp. 15 ff.)

The first attempts to create a monetary union were of mixed success. This was due to the fact that member states of the EEC had been talking early and even negotiated on cooperation in the field of monetary policy, adequate monetary stability (e.g. Bretton Woods), but regularly ensured, that memoranda on this subject have been repeatedly put on hold. Officially, however, the year 1962 and the European Commission document, the so-called Marjolin Memorandum, can be considered as the most appropriate starting point. Based on this document, the first discussions on monetary integration took place at community level, and it came to the first, albeit very limited, measures in the field of monetary cooperation (ibid.). In the context of European unification and the creation of conditions for a common monetary policy, the European System of Central Banks (ESCB) was established. In this system, there are the National Central Banks (NCBs) of all EU countries and the newly established European Central Bank. The euro area, however, includes the ECB and only those NCBs that have adopted the common currency of the Euro. The most of the tasks of the ESCB are fulfilled by the ECB (ECB 2016d, pp. 12 ff.). The decision-making bodies of the ECB are the Governing Council, the Executive Board and the General Council, whose functions shall be explained below.

Executive Board

The Board is composed of the President, a Vice-President and four other members. The term of office of a Board member is eight years, without the possibility of re-election. The Board of Directors conducts the business of the ECB and takes care of the implementation of decisions of the Governing Council and passes required instructions to the NCBs, which in turn must implement the decisions. The Board itself also specifies the tasks laid on the individual members. A well-known function is the responsibility for the economic analysis, where the corresponding person in charge is usually referred to as Chief Economist. To do so the Executive Board usually meets once a week to fulfill the tasks (Scheller 2004, pp. 153 ff.).

Governing Council

The Governing Council comprises of the members of the Executive Board and the chairman of the national central banks of the member states that participating in the Euro. The Governing Council is the supreme decision-making body of the ECB, and makes decisions by simple majority votes of each voting member. The main tasks of the Governing Council include the definition of the monetary policy of the common currency area and the issuance of guidelines and decisions that are needed to fulfill the tasks assigned. The determination of key interest rates and the provision or reduction of central bank money is also included among the guidelines of monetary policy (ECB 2016d, pp. 16 ff.). The Governing Council of the ECB is comparable to the Federal Open Market Committee of the U.S. (FOMC), which is the highest decision-making body of the FED. However, not all members of the FOMC are entitled to vote. The FOMC consists of the members of the Board of Governors (7 members), 5 voting Federal Reserve Bank presidents and 7 non-voting FED presidents of the states (Federal Reserve 2016b).

General Council of the ECB
The General Council consists of the President of the ECB, the Vice-President of the ECB, and the governors of the NCBs of the 28 EU member states. The main difference to the Governing Council with respect to its composition is that representatives of 9 non-Euro area countries also sit at the table. The General Council is involved in the collection of statistical information and debates on the admission of other countries in the monetary union. The General Council normally meets once a quarter, where a member of the European Commission and the President of the Governing Council can participate in the meetings without the right to vote. The General Council can be considered as a transitional body as it would be dissolved once all EU member states have introduced the Euro (ECB 2016d).

Supervisory Board
The Supervisory Board plans and carries out the ECB's supervisory tasks and usually meets twice a month where it is supported by the Steering Committee. It also proposes draft decisions to the Governing Council under the non-objection procedure (ECB 2016e).

3.2. Principles and Objectives
The principle of independence is the main concept regarding the fulfillment of the tasks of the ECB. This principle is very important compared to other major central banks, especially in regard to the guarantee of fiscal stability of the EU and the integration of candidate countries. The principle of independence can be distinguished into five types of independence (Scheller 2004, pp. 121 ff.).

Article 108 of the treaty establishing the European Community declares the **institutional independence** of the ECB. This article stipulates explicitly that, *"when exercising their powers and carrying out their tasks and duties, neither the ECB nor an NCB nor any member of their decision-making bodies shall seek or take instructions from Community institutions or bodies, from any government of a Member State or from any other body. The Community institutions and bodies and the governments of the Member States undertake to respect this principle and not to seek to influence the members of the decision-making bodies of the ECB or of the national central banks in the performance of their tasks."* (EC Treaty (Maastricht consolidated version), Article 107). Although the article makes it illegal to accept instructions from any body, be it public or private, this article does not preclude an exchange or seeking of information or dialogue with bodies mentioned in the article (Scheller 2004, p. 123). Article 123 of the Lisbon Treaty can also be subsumed under the principle of institutional independence. This article states that the ECB cannot grant loans to public budget, respectively states and therefore the ECB cannot finance deficits in the budget of the community or a Member State (The Lisbon Treaty, Article 123).

The principle of **legal independence** is concluded by the legal personality of the ECB. Its legal independence allows the ECB to take action before the European Court of Justice (ECJ) to protect their rights when they are threatened by a Community institution or a Member State (Scheller 2004, p. 122).

To underpin the institutional independence of the ECB, its statutes should protect the **personal independence** of the members of the decision-making bodies of the ECB. These include inter alia long tenures of managerial staff. According to that, members of the Executive Board have a term of eight years, where a reappointment is not possible and the NCB governors have a term of at least five years, where a reappointment is possible. Moreover, a member of the Governing Council can only be deposed from office for 'serious' reasons at the request of the Governing Council or the Executive Board by the European Court of the Office. This also means that no member of the decision-making bodies of the ECB may be dismissed due to a discretionary decision based on his previous performance of central bank-specific tasks (Scheller 2004, p. 123).

Functional and operational independence shall ensure that the ECB is free to decide regarding the method with which it wants to carry out its mission. Furthermore, the ECB is solely responsible for monetary policy and owns the monopoly of issuing bank notes. This means that no legal tender can be created against the will of the ECB and the ECB thus has complete control over the monetary base in the euro area. To carry out its monetary policy, a wide range of instruments are available. These include normative powers, as well as the right to impose and enforce sanctions, if regulations and decisions of the ECB are transgressed. However, the ECB is bound by article 127, paragraph 1 of the TFEU and the ECB Statute to the defined objectives. Additional mandates must be assessed critically (ibid.)[13].

The ECB has its own budget and can decide on its own about the allocation of its resources. Due to this **financial independence**, private banks have only minimal influence on the ECB. The central banks of the euro zone countries hold 70.39% of the capital of the ECB and have paid it to 100%. Non-euro countries hold 29.61% which is paid only to 3.75%. This equity stake has theoretically no effect on personnel policy at the ECB (ECB 2016f). In addition, the ECB as a supranational organization has privileges and reliefs on the territory of the Member States that are used for its duties. Among other things, it is guaranteed that the premises and archives of the ECB are inviolable and its property and assets untouchable (Scheller 2004, p. 124).

The ECB differs in regard of its principle of independence considerably from other major central banks, for example the FED. The FED is always accountable to the Congress of the United States and almost all forms of monetary policy decisions have to be taken within the context of the economic strategies of the United States (Smartinvestor 2016). But, the ECB differs not only in terms of independence from other central banks. While the ECB also makes its contribution in terms of transparency through regular publication of monthly and annual reports, however, the ECB does not publish minutes

---

[13] The 2004 published publication of the ECB 'The European Central Bank - History, Role and Functions' contained in section '4.1.4 Functional and operational independence' the passage (Scheller 2004, p. 124): *"The ECB Regularly monitors the market for possible circumventions of this prohibition (authors note: public sector financing) involving purchases of public debt on the secondary market."* With the programs 'Securities Markets Program (SMP)', 'Outright Monetary Transactions (OMT)' and 'Public Sector Purchase Program (PSPP)', the ECB itself violates against the principle of public sector financing. Under this premise, the principle of functional and operational independence as it is still taught, must be scrutinized.

after its regular Governing Council meetings. This is also contrary to principles of the FED, which regularly publishes minutes of meetings of the FOMC (FED 2016c). However, the ECB grants insights in their assessments of the economic situation through semi-annual projections (Smartinvestor 2016). Another distinguishing feature of the ECB is supposed to be in the definition of its (main) objective. According to article 105, § 1 of the EC Treaty, the primary objective of the ESCB is to maintain price stability (Scheller 2004, p. 45). Although with this defined mandate of the ECB no other direct responsibility to other objectives is placed. However, the ECB should also support in the fulfilment of the objectives referred to article 2 of the EC Treaty. The objectives mentioned in this Article include *"a harmonious, balanced and sustainable development of economic activities, a high level of employment [...], sustainable and noninflationary growth [and] a high degree of competitiveness and convergence of economic performance [...]"* (EC Treaty (Nice consolidated version), article 2). From a legal perspective, the main objective of price stability represents a distinguishing feature compared to the FED, however, in practice they differ in regard to their objectives only marginally. The established statutory objectives by the FED are stable prices, maximum employment, and moderate long-term interest rates (FED 2016d). Even the latter objective is currently fulfilled by both central banks. To accomplish its objectives, the ECB uses a well-defined monetary policy strategy for the euro area. The first element of this strategy is a quantitative definition of price stability. The ECB defines price stability as a growth of the harmonized consumer price index (HICP) in the euro area, which should be below, but close to two percent per year. Within the second element the ECB analyzes the economic developments comprehensively and systematically. These two elements are essential parts in the two-pillar strategy of the ECB (Bundesbank 2016d, p. 183). The first pillar observes within an economic analysis development of inflation itself and measurements that have an impact on inflation. These include for example, wages, exchange rates, long-term interest rates, price and cost indices, and fiscal policy indicators (ibid.). The economic analysis considers especially short to medium-term risks to price stability. Within the second pillar, the ECB monitors with help of a monetary analysis the correlation between the money supply and price developments in the euro area. In particular, the trend of M3 provides over longer periods of time information for future price developments. The results of the analyses are incorporated in inflation forecasts (ibid.). The results of the economic and monetary analysis are reviewed mutually.

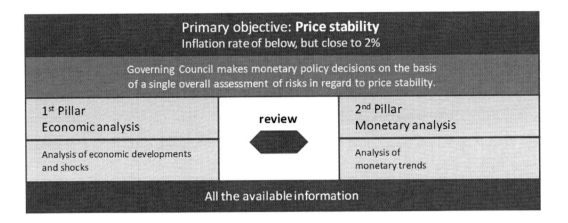

Figure 9: Monetary policy strategy of the euro area
(Illustration by author, data source: Deutsche Bundesbank 2016d, p. 184)

The ECB performs the following tasks that are based on its statutory mandate and the two-pillar strategy (Scheller 2004, p. 48):

- Definition and implementation of monetary policy of the euro area.
- Conduction foreign exchange operations.
- Holding and managing official reserves of euro area Member States.
- Promoting the smooth operation of payment systems.
- The issue of euro banknotes.
- The collection of statistical information.

3.3. Monetary Policy Instruments

According to the ECB, the operational framework consists of open market operations, standing facilities, minimum reserve requirements for credit institutions, and since 2009 asset purchase programs (ECB 2016g). Although monetary policy decisions are made by the ECB, practical implementations are executed operationally by the national central banks. Commercial banks maintain their central bank accounts at the national banks. Open market operations, the management of collateral, and operations in the context of standing facilities are carried out by national banks as well. The ECB may carry out money market transactions bilaterally only in exceptional cases and only with selected counterparties (Deutsche Bundesbank 2016d, p. 187).

Open market operations

The most important open market operation of the ECB is arguably the **main refinancing operations** (MRO), also called main tender. Commercial banks can receive central bank money from the ECB via an auction procedure and the exchange of limited eligible collateral (securities). The central bank money is offered to the highest bidding banks. The minimum bid rate, or main refinancing rate that is fixed by the ECB is often called key interest rate due to its importance. MROs are usually conducted with a frequency and maturity of one week (ECB 2016k).

Longer-term refinancing operations (LTRO) are realized similar to the MROs by repurchase agreements or by mortgage loans. Regular LTROs have a maturity of three months and are conducted each month by the ECB on the basis of standard tenders. Since 2009, the ECB may also conduct non-regular longer-term operations, with a maturity of more than free-months and are called targeted longer-term refinancing operations (TLTRO). Longer-term refinancing operations are liquidity providing and can also serve other monetary policy objectives (ibid.).

Unexpected interest rate deviations and liquidity fluctuations can be compensated with **fine-tuning operations**. They are executed ad hoc primarily as reverse transactions, but may also take the form of foreign exchange swaps, or the collection of fixed-term deposits through quick tenders or bilateral procedures. During these operations, the instruments and procedures are adapted to the types of transaction and the pursued specific objectives (Deutsche Bundesbank 2016d, p. 195).

Structural operations are used to influence the demand of commercial banks on central bank money in the long term. If the demand for central bank money is so low due to special developments that banks hardly depend on refinancing operations, monetary policy instruments cannot operate as desired. The ECB can counteract by selling bonds whereat commercial banks are required to pay the purchase price from their deposits in central bank money, which permanently reduces the stock of central bank money in circulation. In which commercial banks are more dependent to cover their demand for central bank money via weekly refinancing operations. Structural operations are usually carried out by the ECB through reverse transactions, outright transactions, and the issuance of dept certificates (Deutsche Bundesbank 2016d, p. 196).

Standing facilities

There are two standing facilities available to eligible counterparties on their own initiative. The **marginal lending facility** rate provides commercial banks with the possibility to receive liquidity by interest payment and collateral at the ECB until the following business day whereas the corresponding interest rate normally provides a ceiling for the overnight market interest rate. But commercial banks can also deposit their surplus liquidity as demand deposits at the ECB, respectively NCBs until next business day at the interest rate of the **deposit facility** in the form of overnight money. This interest rate normally provides a floor for the overnight market interest rate (Deutsche Bundesbank 2016d, p. 198).

The following illustration shows the development of the mentioned interest rates that are issued by the ECB.

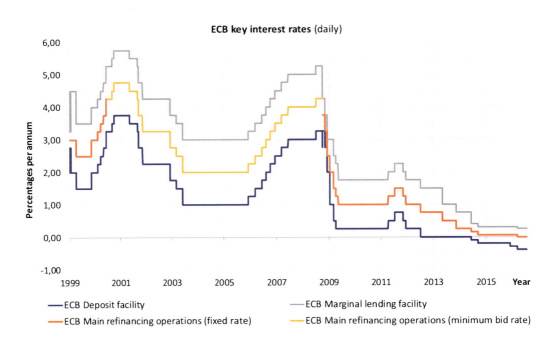

Figure 10: Key interest rates issued by the ECB
(Illustration by author, data source: Statistical Data Warehouse of the ECB 2016a)

The carrying out of the MROs from 28.06.2000 until 15.10.2008 was based on a variable interest rate, where the quoted interest rate was the minimum interest rate for offering. Since 15.10.2008, the ECB carries the MROs out again as a fixed rate tender (ECB 2016j).

Minimum reserves

The ECB requires commercial banks to hold minimum reserves on accounts with the national central banks. The amount of reserve results from liabilities subject to reserve requirements of a commercial bank, measured at the end of selected months. Subject to reserve are for example overnight customer deposits, debt securities with an agreed maturity of up to two years and money market securities. These subject to reserve liabilities are multiplied by the reserve ratio. The reserve period typically lasts 42 or 49 days since 2015 and starts each Wednesday following the monetary policy Governing Council meeting. The reserves held by the ECB are remunerated by the ECB to the average interest rate of the main refinancing operations. Minimum reserves in contrast to main refinancing operations and standing facilities represent rather a regulatory than a monetary policy instrument. The ECB reduced the minimum reserve ratio due to financial and economic uncertainties in January 2012 from 2% to 1% (Deutsche Bundesbank 2016d, p. 189). The following illustration provides an overview about the monetary developments of the aforementioned monetary policy instruments conducted by the ECB. The volume of transactions shown in the graph are not summed up or stacked.

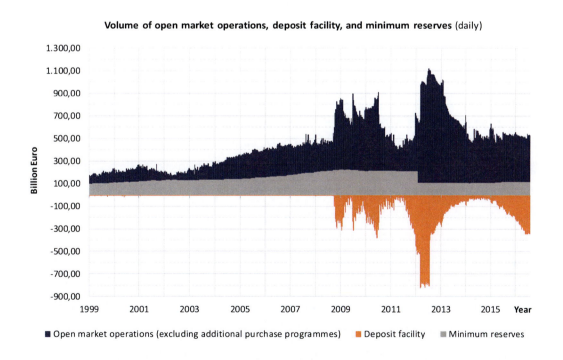

Figure 11: Vol. of open market operations, deposit facility, and minimum reserves held with the ECB
(Illustration by author, data source ECB 2016i)

Foreign exchange intervention

The ECB intervenes occasionally on the foreign exchange market to stabilize its monetary policy or to support its sales policy. It should be noted that foreign exchange interventions are not officially mentioned as instrument by the ECB. Such interventions are conducted either unilaterally or as part of a coordinated intervention involving other central banks. Foreign exchange interventions are only used, when there are large and misguiding exchange rate movements that may jeopardize either the inflation target or the economic stability of the euro area (ECB 2016h).

Asset purchase programs

The ECB decided in the wake of the banking, financial and sovereign crisis to implement in addition to its interest rate policy and full allotment further special measures to counteract the negative effects of the crisis. According to the general rules on monetary policy instruments and procedures of the euro area, outright transactions on markets are a component of the monetary policy framework of the ECB. These operations are only intended to be used to adjust structural liquidity positions of the financial sector against the euro area. There are currently several transactions in the framework of different asset purchase programs (APP) (Deutsche Bundesbank 2016f). These programs should resolve either disturbances on the securities markets or lower long-term interest rates in the context of quantitative easing (QE) to achieve the ECBs objective of price stability. This in turn should revive the demand from businesses and consumers for loans in order that the economy gains momentum. Accordingly, inflation would rise and approach the targeted value of the central bank (Deutsche Bundesbank 2016d, p. 206). In the following, active and completed programs are described.

Covered bond purchase program 1,2,3 (CBPP1, CBPP2, CBPP3)

Between July 2009 and June 2010, the ECB purchased covered bonds within the framework of CBPP1 of about 60 billion Euros. Between November 2011 and October 2010, the ECB purchased again covered bonds within CBPP2 of about 16 billion Euros. The ECB intends to hold the assets bought under CBPP1 and CBPP2 until maturity. In October 2014, the ECB started within a third row to purchase covered bonds to an intended amount of EUR 60 billion per month until March 2017th (extended). However, the EUR 60 billion are coupled or shared with the

ABSPP and PSPP programme. Compared to CBPP1 and CBPP2, the ECB buys under CBPP3 bonds on the secondary and primary market (ECB 2016g, Deutsche Bundesbank 2016e). These purchase programs should aim at the support of the respective market segment, the easing of the funding conditions for credit institutions and companies (an improvement in the supply of credit in general), as well as to improve the monetary policy transmission process (ECB 2016g).

Securities markets program (SMP)

In May 2010, the ECB started purchasing securities in the context of the SMP to counteract disturbances in the monetary policy transmission mechanism.[14] Until September 2012, securities were purchased by the ECB in the amount of 219 billion Euros. The liquidity that was provided by this program was absorbed by weekly operations after its discontinuation until June 2014. The securities in the SMP portfolio will be held to maturity (ECB 2016g).

Asset-backed securities purchase program (ABSPP)

Since November 2014, the ECB purchases asset-backed securities within the ABSPP for at least two years. The ABSPP shares its purchase volume of about EUR 60 billion per mount with the CBPP3 and PSPP. It is intended that this program helps banks to diversify funding sources and should stimulate the issuance of new securities. Like the CSPP it should furthermore help the transmission of the ECBs monetary policy (ECB 2016g).

Public sector purchase program (PSPP)

Within the framework of the PSPP, the ECB purchases since March 2015 public sector securities. These securities include nominal and inflation-linked central government bonds and bonds issued by recognized agencies, regional and local governments, international organizations and multilateral development banks located in the euro area (ECB 2016g). The purchases take place only on the secondary market. The PSPP is also a part of the EUR 60 billion program that

---

[14] The mentioned disturbances in the monetary policy transmission mechanism refer in general to the European debt crisis, that started in 2009. In spring 2010, the situation escalated dramatically when Greece could no longer conceal the extent of his hitherto veiled budget deficits and its height of debt. The interest rates on Greek government bonds had become unaffordable for Greece. On 23 April 2010 Greece had to apply for grants in order to avert a sovereign default (Landeszentrale für politische Bildung Baden-Württemberg 2016).

consists of the CBPP3 and ABSPP and should at least run until September 2016. In March 2016, the ECB announced that it will increase the joint program by EUR 20 billion through purchases within the PSPP and its extension until March 2017. With this programme, the ECB states that it wants to counteract a too long-lasting phase of low inflation with this program (ibid.).

Corporate Sector Purchase Program (CSPP)

In March 2016, the Governing Council of the ECB announced to supplement the APP by the purchase of Euro-denominated investment grade bonds of companies. Within this programme, the ECB may purchase bonds issued by non-banks located in the euro area. The corporate sector purchase program will contribute to the APP's total monthly purchase volume of now EUR 80 billion (ECB 2016g), although the purchase volumes will not be published ex-ante. The purchases started in June 2016 and are carried out at the primary and the secondary market. This program should provide further monetary policy accommodation (ibid.).

Outright Monetary Transactions (OMT)

In September 2012, the ECB announced a program with which it is possible to purchase to an unlimited extent short-term bonds issued by states in the euro area. Such purchases will only take place on the condition that the state concerned shall submit to the requirements of the EFSF-/ESM-program (Deutsche Bundesbank 2016e). Additional technical characteristics were set by the ECB that caused until today, that the necessary preconditions for the implementation of the program are not fulfilled by any state within the euro area. Purchases have not been made until today (status: August 2016). However, it is generally assumed that even the mere announcement in the past has had a calming or interest-lowering effect on the financial markets (The Economist 2016).

The following illustration provides an overview of the development of holdings by the euro area of securities held for monetary policy purposes from January 2009 until August 2016. These additional special measures were launched in the wake of the financial and economic crisis. The ECB provides for much of these asset purchase programs a consolidated overview about the purchases and holdings on its webpage. However, the holdings for the SMP are not listed separately before 2014. Nevertheless, they can be calculated by using the balance sheet of the ECB which is available from the statistical data warehouse of the ECB. The corresponding values in figure 12 are calculated between May 2010 and January 2014 by subtracting the values for CBPP 1 and 2 from the sum of all securities held for monetary policy purposes. The volume of transactions shown in the graph are stacked, resp. summed up. The illustration shows additionally the development of inflation in the euro area, since price stability is the primary objective of the ECB. This objective targets an inflation rate of approximately 2%. The majority of APPs was established to counteract a too long-lasting phase of inflation. The values of inflation are plotted on the secondary axis.

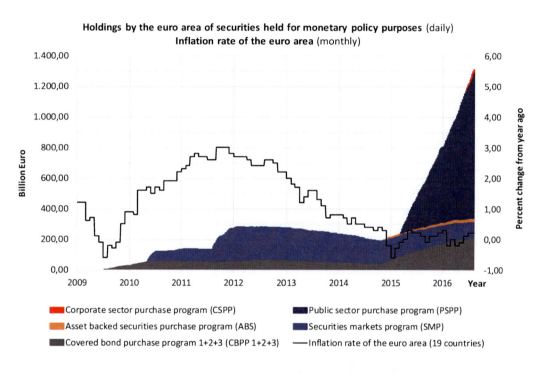

Figure 12: Holdings by the ECB of securities held for monetary policy purpose
(Illustration by author, data source: ECB 2016i)

4. Interest Levels and Savings Behavior

It is important for a qualitative analysis of interest rate developments to answer the following question: What can be considered a 'normal' level of interest rates? The answer to this question is for the study of central importance. The following sections therefore deals with the distinction of interest by taking into account its nominal value and the development of inflation. A brief introduction into the topic of saving behavior under the premises of interest rate developments and types of investments should open the course of the examination in chapter 5.

4.1. Nominal Interest Rate

The interest rate specified in percentage of the nominal value of a bond or a loan that a bank or credit institution would quote, is usually called nominal interest rate and indicates how fast the amount of money rises over time (Mankiw 2006, p. 497). This interest rate is charged or paid in the market and is therefore also called market interest rate, because this rate is often realized through the interaction of the demand for and supply of loanable funds (Arnold 2008, p. 306). The nominal interest rate is reported without a correction for the effects of costs or changes in purchasing power (Mankiw 2006, p. 497). The interest rate for a specified period generally corresponds to the following ratio (Güida 2009, p. 242):

$$nominal\ interst\ rate = \frac{(initial\ capital + interest\ inome) - initial\ capital}{initial\ capital}$$

Key interest rates, which are set unilaterally by a central bank as part of its monetary policy and to conduct business with its affiliated credit institutions are a nominal rate. Although settlement costs and fees are not incorporated in the notion of the interest rates, expected inflation, however, is taken into account within the process of interest formation, because inflation plays a decisive role in the central bank's monetary policy.[15] Key interest rates are therefore not adjusted for inflation.

---

[15] The context between (expected) inflation and the determination of key interest rates is particularly important regarding the so-called Taylor rule. The rule was first proposed by John B. Taylor and represents an empirical approach that is based on economic studies. The general objective of this rule is the determination of the monetary policy and key interest rates that are set by central banks. The Taylor rule can be considered as a guide to action for central banks and includes expected inflation within the calculation (Koenig 2012).

The following illustration provides an overview of the development of nominal key interest rates since 1999 in the euro area, USA, and Japan. Due to their importance and general perception, the following key interest rates are chosen in the illustration: ECB main refinancing operations rate (fixed and flexible), the Federal funds target rate and range of the U.S., and the overnight call rate of the Bank of Japan.

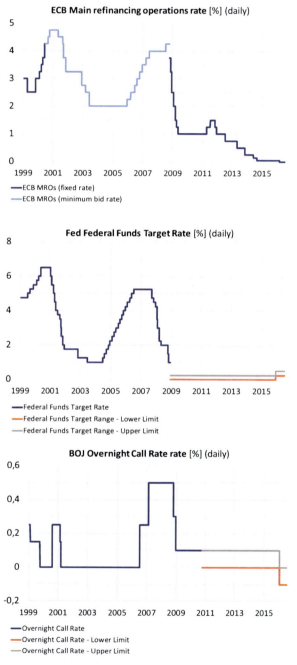

Figure 13: Key interest rates of the euro area, USA, Japan
(Illustration by author, data source: ECB 2016j, Federal Bank of St. Louis 2016c, Bankenverband 2016)

4.2. Real Interest Rate

If the nominal interest rate is adjusted for the effects of inflation, the resulting inflation-adjusted rate is called real interest rate (Mankiw 2006, p. 497). The real interest rate must be distinguished from the effective interest rate. The latter includes in addition to the inflation-adjusted real interest rate all incurred costs, such as account administration charges (Güida 2009, p. 242). It is important to correct economic variables like interest rates for the effects of inflation. If, for example, the rate of inflation exceeds the rate of interest that is paid on an investment, the purchasing power actually falls. This context can be derived generally from the so-called Fisher equation. This equation is named after Irving Fisher (1867-1947) who first studied the relationship between inflation, nominal and real interest rate (Mankiw 2015, p. 645). His equation provides a definition for the real interest rate within an economy in terms of the nominal interest rate and the expected inflation rate. The Fisher effect that can be derived from its equation states, that under certain assumptions a change in the inflation rate is proportional transferred to the nominal interest rate.[16]

The relation Fisher postulated can be noted as follows (Teall 2013, p. 190):

i_n = nominal interest rate
i_r = real interest rate
π^e_{t+1} = expected inflation

$$(1 + i_n) = (1 + i_r) \cdot (1 + \pi^e_{t+1}) \qquad (4.2.1)$$

By multiplying out the term of the right side of the equation and approximation with the assumption that the inflation rate is low follows:

$$(1 + i_n) = 1 + i_r + \pi^e_{t+1} + i_r \cdot \pi^e_{t+1}$$

$$\Rightarrow i \approx i_r + \pi^e_{t+1}$$

---

[16] The strict separation of monetary and real economy in the context of the classic dichotomy is significant in Fisher's theory. According to this, the real interest rate of the capital market is determined as the interest rate that compensates for savings and demand for capital goods. Monetary factors are irrelevant for the determination of the real interest rate. Changes in the inflation rate cannot affect the real interest rate and are reflected directly in the nominal interest rate. Moreover, the Fisher effect assumes perfect foresight, a perfect market, perfect market transparency and zero transactions costs (Anderegg 2007, p. 160).

In contrast to the nominal interest rate, inflation expectations and real interest rates are not observable quantities. Inflation expectation is therefore not a final quantity and is derived from the values of the past. But the real interest rate for a certain period can be determined approximately by using the ex-post real interest rate π_{t+1}. Expected inflation will be replaced by the actual inflation rate, which, however, is only known ex-post. In this case, it must be assumed that there are no systematic expectation errors on the inflation rate (Croushore 2015, p. 133 ff.). It is also possible to calculate the real interest rate by taking into account taxes. The after-tax realized real interest rate is calculated as follows (ibid.):

i_n = nominal interest rate
i_r = real interest rate
π_{t+1} = ex-post inflation
τ_g = capital gains tax rate

$$i_r = \left(\frac{i_n \cdot (1 - \tau_g) - \pi_{t+1}}{1 + \pi_{t+1}} \right) \qquad (4.2.2)$$

According to monetary theory there are different forces that determine each of the two terms of the right side of equation no. 4.2.1. As shown in chapter 2, the supply and demand for loanable funds determine the real interest rate and growth in the money supply determines the inflation rate. In the short-run, a change in the money does not affect the real interest rate. Therefore, the nominal interest rate must adjust one-for-one to changes in the inflation rate (Mankiw 2015, p. 645). This assumption is used when a central bank increases the rate of money growth and expects in the long-run a higher inflation rate and a higher nominal interest rate. The close association between these two variables can be verified empirically in almost every country in the western hemisphere (ibid.).

The following illustration provides an overview about the development of inflation in the euro area and the most important key interest rate, the MRO lending rate of the ECB from January 1999 until July 2016. The real interest rate is also shown in the graph, where the following equation was used with the parameters from equation 4.2.1 and 4.2.2:

$$i_r = \left(\frac{i_n - \pi_{t+1}}{1 + \pi_{t+1}} \right)$$

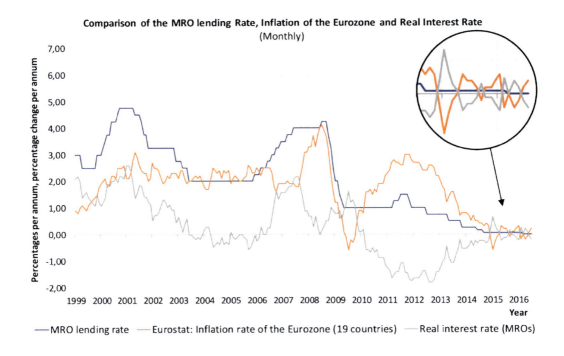

Figure 14: The development of inflation, the MRO lending rate,
and the real interest rate within the euro area
(Illustration by author, data source: ECB 2016j, Statistical Data Warehouse of the ECB 2016b)

4.3. Savings Behavior

Spurred by the current low interest levels, the question is often asked in the public debate whether saving at all is still worthwhile. This study contributes to answer this question by analyzing the current real interest rate levels. Next to the development of interest rates for certain asset classes, the savings behavior plays a decisive role, especially regarding the formation of implications based on the evaluation results from chapter 5. It has to be differentiated in this context between private saving, national saving, and public saving (Mankiw 2015, p. 555). For this study, only private saving is taken into account. According to Mankiw (2015), private saving is *"[...] the income that households have left after paying for taxes and consumption."*. It is typically distinguished between purpose savings and retirement savings (Gabler Economic Lexicon 2016b). Regardless of the reason savings are created, the goal is always the creation of a financial reserve for future expenses. The percentage of the amount of savings from the disposable income of a household is called the household savings rate. With this measurement, international comparisons can be made. From the latest available data from the

Organisation for Economic Co-operation and Development (OECD), the euro area has a household saving rate of 5,96% in 2014, which is in the midfield of the OECD countries. Germany has typically one of the highest saving rates in the euro area (2012: 10,3%), Spain one of the lowest (2012: 4,4%) and Luxembourg the highest (2012: 13,7%) (OECD 2014).[17] But, there are big differences within Europe not only in terms of the savings rate. Distinctions can also be made in the context of risk awareness and habits. Germany is traditionally one of the most conservative countries regarding risk appetite for investments worldwide (Heilmann et al. 2014, p. 15; Bank of Scotland 2015). The following illustration provides an overview about the structure and amount per capita of gross financial assets of Germany, Spain and Luxembourg in 2014.

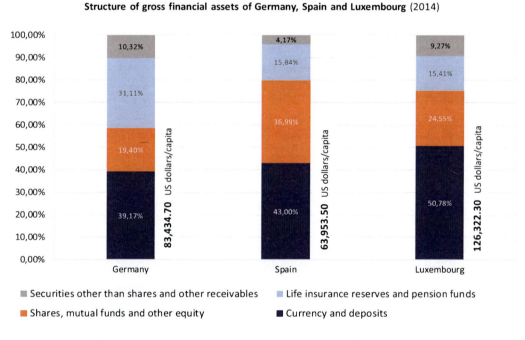

Figure 15: Structure of gross financial assets of selected countries
(Illustration by author, data source: OECD 2016b)

---

[17] In 2012, Luxembourg had the highest household net saving rate of 13.7%, Germany a saving rate of 10.3%, and Spain 4.4%. However, the saving rates vary over the years compared very strong. The savings rate of Luxembourg had more than tripled between 2006 und 2012, the saving rate of Spain between 2006 and 2009 as well, but halved again between 2009 and 2012. The saving rate of Germany fluctuated between 1999 and 2012 only by about 16% (OECD 2014).

5. The Development of Yield Levels

The following study analyzes the development of yield levels of selected asset classes from 1999-2016 within the sphere of influence of the ECB. Since distinctive rate cuts of key interest rates and the extension of asset purchase programs by the ECB, several studies tried to predict the impact of these measurements on yield levels for Germany, or, more recently, analyzed the impact empirically (Schneider, Thesling 2015, Faber 2010). But, there is a lack of ambition perceptible to examine the issue within the framework of a European consciousness. For this reason, this study analyses the development of yield levels of Germany, Spain and Luxembourg. The selection of countries was made under the premises of inflation, government debt, and the households saving behavior. The corresponding value on the upper side, the lower side as well as the middle were considered in the selection process. The following table shows the relevant placements of the countries and the corresponding values in brackets.

Rank	Government debt as percent of GDP 2015	Rank	Inflation rate 2015 [%]	Rank	Household saving rate 2012 [%]
6.	Spain (99,17)	8.	Germany (0,1)	1.	Luxembourg (13,7)
:		:		:	
11.	Germany (71,15)	12.	Luxembourg (0,1)	3.	Germany (10,3)
:		:		:	
18.	Luxemourg (21,44)	15.	Spain (-0,6)	7.	Spain (4,4)

Table 5: Selection criteria for the chosen countries and their placements within the euro area
(Illustration by author, data source: Eurostat 2016, OECD 2016c, OECD 2014)

Inflation plays a decisive for role to calculate real interest rates. If this rate does not differ significantly among the countries of the euro area, which was the case for 2015, the most important criterion was its leading sign whether it is positive or negative. The household saving rate is a criterion within the evaluation of the results of the study. It is possible to infer which countries are the most affected regarding changes of real interest rates. Government debt as percent of GDP is also a criterion within the evaluation of the results. For this reason, asset purchase programs are considered during the evaluation as well. As shown in chapter 3.3, within the framework of the most purchase programs, the ECB buys government bonds and thus affects indirectly, and in some cases even directly the government debt of member countries of the euro area.

Figure 16: Development of inflation in Germany, Spain and Luxembourg from 1999-2016 (Illustration by author, data source: Eurostat 2016)

The selection of asset classes was mainly made under the premises of maturity and the accessibility by people. Debt securities issued by the corresponding countries with a 10 years' maturity are chosen as an equivalent for long-term interest rates. This interest rate is, for example, a component of the yield on bonds outstanding, which is issued by the German National Bank (Deutsche Bundesbank 2016g). Bank interest rates on deposits from households with an agreed maturity of over one and up to two years are chosen as an equivalent for short-term interest rates on savings. These interest rates are issued by monetary financial institutions (MFI), except central banks and money market funds. Further criteria were new business coverage and the denomination in Euro. New business coverage was used as a criterion, because these rates reflect a change in key interest rates most likely. All data were obtained from the statistical data warehouse of the ECB. Appendix 1 provides an overview about the raw data and additional information about its availability. The methodology of data acquisition and data processing is available on the homepage of the statistical data warehouse of the ECB: http://sdw.ecb.europa.eu. The stock market is in addition to fixed-income securities and bonds also an important investment opportunity. As shown in chapter 4.3, the proportion of shares or mutual funds is almost 20% of gross financial assets in Germany. For this reason, the development of appropriate share price indices was also taken into account. The corresponding data were obtained from the OECD. The data for each country was normalized by the OECD to the reference period of 2010 with a reference amount of 100 in order to ensure comparability. The calculated index measures how the value of the stocks in the index is changing. This index is comparable to the corresponding national benchmark index of each country (DAX30 for Germany, IBEX35 for Spain, LuxX for Luxembourg). Detailed information about the statistical concept of the indices is shown in Appendix 2. An annual yield was calculated (year over year, yoy), for each index, respectively country. The corresponding month 12 months before each month was used as the beginning of the investment cycle. In doing so, the value of each month was put in ratio to the month 12 months before.

The aspect of comparability was another criterion within the selection process of the chosen interest rates. Every country has a particular national interest, that is most relevant for national investigations, e.g. yield on bonds outstanding in Germany. Such interest rates differ among the selected countries. For this reason, interest rates that are available from the statistical data warehouse of the ECB and the OECD were used, which enable comparability most likely. The following listing recaps the relevant countries and the studied variables.

Countries
- Germany
- Spain
- Luxembourg

Asset Classes
- Long-term interest rates with a maturity of 10 years.
  (during the study also named: Long-term interest rates)

- Bank interest rates on deposits with an agreed maturity of over one and up to two years.
  (during the study also named: Bank interest rates)
- Return on share price index, year over year.
  (during the study also named: Return on share price index.)

The development of the interest rate of the respective asset class was subsequently investigated. The real interest rate was calculated for each asset class and country. The corresponding detailed values for the countries and asset classes can be found in Appendix 3, including tax adjusted values and a graphical illustration in Appendix 5.[18] The data for inflation comes directly from Eurostat. The inflation rate for each country was calculated as the annual rate of change of the HICP for the corresponding country (Eurostat 2016)[19]. Due to a varying availability of data, different periods have been used for the asset classes. Long-term interest rates were analyzed from January 1999 until July 2016, bank interest rates on deposits from January 2000 until June 2016 (Luxembourg from January 2003 – June 2016) and the return on share price indices from January 2001 until July 2016. Nevertheless, the time periods with exactly 16 or approximately 16 years are large enough to investigate the impact of monetary policy activities by the ECB since its implementation of a Pan-European monetary policy in 1999. In addition to the real interest rate developments, it was investigated, to what extent nominal and inflation-adjusted interest rate developments correlate with the MRO lending rate of the ECB. In this context, it was also examined to what extent a more pronounced correlation with the asset purchase programs exist. All asset purchase programs were taken into account that were implemented for monetary policy purposes since 2009. Figure 12 on page 53 shows the named programs with their corresponding amounts.

---

[18] For tax adjustment the following capital income tax rates were applied: Germany 30,5% (25% plus 5.5% solidarity surcharge), Spain: 19% on the first EUR 6,000 of savings, Luxembourg: 10% on Luxembourg-source interest received (Bundeszentralamt für Steuern 2016, Angloinfo 2016, EP Services 2016).

[19] The Eurostat data code identification is *prc_hicp_manr*.

5.1. Methodology of the Empirical Study

Formula 4.2.1 was used for the calculation of the real interest rate. The already occurred inflation rate was used, although the formula uses in its original version the expected inflation rate. This is reasonable, because the realized real interest rate is examined and long-term interest rates can only be determined with uncertainty about the expected inflation rate. For this reason, the ex-post real interest rate was calculated, which is a common practice for scientific studies (Blanchard, Illing 2019, p. 422). The subsequent determination of the correlation of asset classes with the key interest rate requires some preconditions. The most frequently used Pearson correlation coefficient requires an interval scale of the analyzed values and linearity of the dependency. For a subsequent verification of the significance, a normal distribution of the variable in the population and homoscedasticity is necessary (Schäfer 2016, p. 101). Homoscedasticity means that the variance of the residuals is not significantly different for all occurrences of the other variables (Hackl 2005, p. 46). While linearity can be checked visually in the scatter diagram, the assumption of homoscedasticity can be checked in the plot of residuals versus predicted values (Boston University School of Public Health 2016). To confirm homoscedasticity, the plotted values should be approximately evenly distributed around the zero line. Equal distribution can be verified by using the Kolmogorov-Smirnov or the Shapiro-Wilks test. However, both tests have often rejected the existence of an equal distribution in the verification process of the variables in this study. Due to a large number of values even very small deviations from the normal distribution can be significant and therefore cause a rejection of the normal distribution by tests (Möller 2011, p. 138). This phenomenon is known as law of large numbers. For this reason, an alternative verification process was used and the skewness and kurtosis were examined. If the values of skewness and kurtosis are between -1 to +1, it can be reasonably assumed that the data is normally distributed (ibid.). This approach was used during the study because of the large sample size (>200).

The correlation coefficient can calculate values between -1 and 1. A correlation coefficient of 0 means that there is no relationship between two variables. A correlation coefficient of +1 describes a perfect positive correlation between two variables, while a correlation of -1 describes a perfect inverse correlation. The Pearson correlation is calculated by the following formula (Augustin 2014, p. 21):

$$\rho_{X,Y} = \frac{\text{cov}(X,Y)}{\sigma_X \cdot \sigma_Y} = \frac{\sum_{i=1}^{n}(X_i - \bar{X}) \cdot (Y_i - \bar{Y})}{\sqrt{\sum_{i=1}^{n}(X_i - \bar{X})^2 \cdot \sum_{i=1}^{n}(Y_i - \bar{Y})^2}} \qquad (5.1.1)$$

X, Y = variables
$\text{cov}(X,Y)$ = covariance of X,Y
σ = standard deviation
$E(x)$ = expected value of x

However, the evaluation of the data for this study has shown, that the preconditions for the validity of the Pearson correlation are rarely met. To ensure comparability, two nonparametric correlation coefficients were additionally calculated, which can be used if the data is not normally distributed and/or the connection is not linear (Keller 2013). The first correlation coefficient that was calculated in addition to the Pearson correlation coefficient is the Spearman's rank correlation coefficient (Spearman's rho). This coefficient can also calculate values between -1 and +1. Spearman's Rho is a rank correlation coefficient and measures how well an arbitrary monotonic function can describe the relationship between two variables, without making any assumptions about the probability distribution of the variables. The coefficient is calculated by the following formula (Augustin 2014, p. 22):

$$\rho_{X,Y} = \frac{\text{cov}(rg_x, rg_y)}{s_{rg_x} \cdot s_{rg_y}} \qquad (5.1.2)$$

x, y = variables
$rg(x_i)$ = rank of x
s_{rg_z} = standard deviation of the ranks of x
$\text{cov}(rg(x), rg(y))$ = covariance of rg(x) and rg(y)

The third correlation coefficient is called Kendall rank correlation coefficient (Kendall's tau) and bases on the concept of concordant and discordant ranks. The coefficient compares all possible combinations of pairs of values with one another. This coefficient is considered as the superior level compared with Spearman's Rho among many statisticians. The coefficient is calculated by the following formula (Augustin 2014, p. 22):

$$\tau = \frac{(\textit{number of concordant pairs}) - (\textit{number of discordant pairs})}{\frac{1}{2} \cdot N \cdot (N-1)} \qquad (5.1.3)$$

N = number of pairs

The significance of the correlation coefficient was calculated by using the t-statistic:

$$t = \frac{|r|}{\sqrt{\frac{1-r^2}{N-2}}} \qquad (5.1.4)$$

t = test quantity of t-distribution
N = sample size (number of measuring points)
r = Pearson correlation coefficient

The occurrence of autocorrelation was also examined. Its intensity was calculated by using the Durbin-Watson test. This test is a common procedure to examine autocorrelation (Faber 2010, p. 143). The valuation parameters are: d=2, which means no autocorrelation; d=0, which means perfect positive autocorrelation; and d=4, which means perfect negative autocorrelation. Autocorrelation describes the correlation of a function or a signal with itself at an earlier time. The Durbin-Watson test is calculated by using the following formula (Western Carolina University 2016):

$$d = \frac{\sum_{t=2}^{T}(\varepsilon_t - \varepsilon_{t-1})^2}{\sum_{t=1}^{T} \varepsilon_t^2} \qquad (5.1.5)$$

ε_t = residuals of regression in period t

The calculations of the evaluation were performed in Excel and by using the statistics program IBM® SPSS® Statistics, Version 24. Appendix 4 provides the detailed results of the investigation of each asset class and country.

5.2. The Development of Yield Levels in Germany

The following chart shows the development of inflation-adjusted long-term interest rates with a maturity of 10 years, inflation-adjusted bank interest rates on deposits with an agreed maturity of over 1 and up to 2 years, and the inflation-adjusted return on the share price index in Germany. The interest rate for the return on the share price index is plotted on the secondary axis and the levels of the MRO lending rate are shown blue shaded.

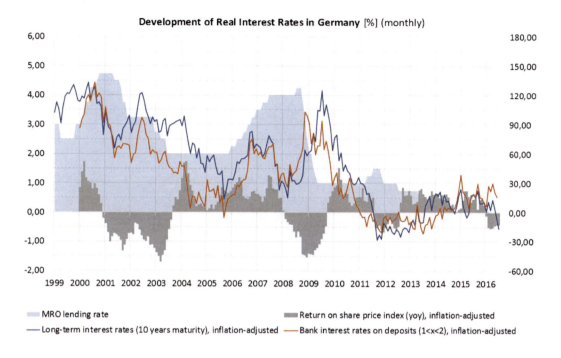

Figure 17: Development of real interest rates in Germany
(Illustration by author, data source: ECB 2016j, Eurostat 2016,
Statistical Data Warehouse of the ECB 2016b, OECD 2016d)

The diagram shows, that inflation-adjusted long-term interest rates have negative values of about -0.50% since the middle of 2016 in Germany. However, in the second half of 2011, the inflation-adjusted interest rate on long-term debt securities was at almost -1.00%, which was the most negative value within the past 16 years. In 2014 and 2015, the values were almost completely in positive terrain. Furthermore, the values of inflation adjusted long-term interest rates varied between +4.40% and -1.00% since 1999. The same applies approximately to bank interest rates on deposits. Though, the most negative value can be observed in the middle of 2013 of about -0.80%. Moreover, this interest rate has inflation-adjusted positive values since 2014. The magnitude of this inflation-adjusted interest rate in 2015 or 2016 is comparable to the level of 2004 or 2005. The return on shares, however, fluctuates exorbitant compared to the other two interest rates. This is not surprising, because stock markets are considered in general as great opportunity for capital gains, but also as very risky. The diagram shows evidence for a positive correlation of long-term interest rates and bank interest rates on deposits with the MRO interest rate of the ECB.

The following table shows the results of the correlation evaluation. An evaluation of the correlation of the inflation-adjusted return on share prices with the MRO lending rate was omitted. The corresponding evaluation results from the nominal values indicate not a correlation, and the significance level indicates also a discard of the values. Furthermore, because of its magnitude a significant change of the nominal values of the return on share prices through inflation cannot be expected.

nominal interest rate	Correlation with MRO lending rate (1999-2016)					
	Pearson product-moment correlation coefficient	Significance (two-sided)	Kendall rank correlation coefficient	Significance (two-sided)	Spearman's rank correlation coefficient	Significance (two-sided)
Long-term interest rates	0,877	yes (0.1 level)	0,748	yes (0.1 level)	0,901	yes (0.1 level)
Bank interest rates on deposits	0,969	yes (0.1 level)	0,896	yes (0.1 level)	0,976	yes (0.1 level)
Return on share price index	0,259	no (0,250)	-0,046	no (0,356)	-0,091	no (0,200)
inflation-adjusted interest rate	Pearson product-moment correlation coefficient	Significance (two-sided)	Kendall rank correlation coefficient	Significance (two-sided)	Spearman's rank correlation coefficient	Significance (two-sided)
Long-term interest rates	0,620	yes (0.1 level)	0,442	yes (0.1 level)	0,642	yes (0.1 level)
Bank interest rates on deposits	0,722	yes (0.1 level)	0,499	yes (0.1 level)	0,703	yes (0.1 level)

Table 6: Correlation of yield levels in Germany with the MRO lending rate
(Illustration by author, data source: ECB 2016j, Eurostat 2016,
Statistical Data Warehouse of the ECB 2016b, OECD 2016d)

The evaluated data does not fulfill the preconditions at all times for the applicability of the Pearson correlation coefficient for all three countries. The interpretation of the results is therefore carried out on the basis of the rank correlation coefficients. As expected, the correlation of the chosen nominal interest rates with the MRO lending rate is significant. The same applies to the correlation of inflation-adjusted interest rates, although the correlation coefficients have considerably lower values. This makes sense, because the key interest rates are determined by taking into account inflation. In this case, the real interest rate has fewer attributes that determine its value.

The evaluation furthermore shows, that there is possibly no correlation of the return on share prices in Germany to the main key interest rate of the ECB. This result is surprising, because the monetary theory implies a considerably different outcome. But, this finding is well known amongst traders in the financial market regarding German stocks. Stock markets can at least in Germany perform a parallel upward movement in an environment of rising key interest rates (manager magazin 2014).

The Durbin-Watson test shows a value of about 0,081 for the nominal values and a value of 0,288 for the inflation-adjusted values. Both values indicate clearly the existence of autocorrelation. This phenomenon is typical for market interest rates (Faber 55). This can be explained, inter alia through the appearance of herding. Herding means, that market participants imitate the behavior of other market participants and ignore deliberately own information. In this case, price movements can intensify itself through their own degree of strength in price movements (ibid.).

The following table shows the results of the correlation evaluation of the nominal interest rates with the asset purchase programs by the ECB.

nominal interest rate	Correlation with asset purchase programs (2009-2016)					
	Pearson product-moment correlation coefficient	Significance (two-sided)	Kendall rank correlation coefficient	Significance (two-sided)	Spearman's rank correlation coefficient	Significance (two-sided)
Long-term interest rates	-0,745	yes (0.1 level)	-0,618	yes (0.1 level)	-0,801	yes (0.1 level)
Bank interest rates on deposits	-0,605	yes (0.1 level)	-0,355	yes (0.1 level)	-0,569	yes (0.1 level)
Return on share price index	0,385	yes (0.1 level)	-0,210	yes (0.1 level)	-0,300	yes (0.1 level)

Table 7: Correlation of yield levels in Germany with asset purchase programs by the ECB
(Illustration by author, data source: ECB 2016j, Eurostat 2016,
Statistical Data Warehouse of the ECB 2016b, OECD 2016d)

As expected, the evaluation shows a strong correlation of nominal interest rates of long-term debt securities and bank deposits to the asset purchase programs by the ECB, but reverse. The reason is an opposite development of the summed asset purchases. However, it is difficult to present a causal explanation about the difference in intensity of the correlation compared to the correlation with the MRO lending rate. In this case, the exact amount of German securities should be used that is purchased by the ECB. For this reason, the correlation in figure 20 indicates not exactly a proportional connection, because under the current main purchase program, the ECB purchases bonds in proportion to each euro area country's economy and population (Fairless 2016).

5.3. The Development of Yield Levels in Spain

The following illustration shows the development of the inflation-adjusted interest rates in Spain. The explanatory notes to the diagram of Germany apply here as well.

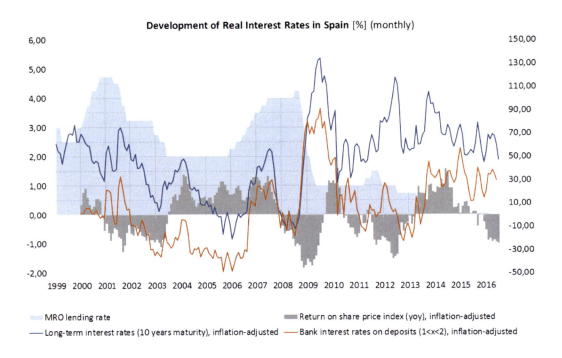

Figure 18: Development of real interest rates in Spain
(Illustration by author, data source: ECB 2016j, Eurostat 2016,
Statistical Data Warehouse of the ECB 2016b, OECD 2016d)

The diagram shows, that inflation-adjusted interest rates for long-term debt securities and bank deposits have positive values in Spain since 2013. The diagram shows impressively the impact of the latest financial crisis and that especially long-term interest rates in Spain, even inflation-adjusted are at a considerably higher level compared to Germany. Nevertheless, Spain had also experienced a period with negative inflation-adjusted interest rates. Between 2002 and 2006, bank interest rates on deposits were inflation-adjusted consistently in negative territory. In 2005, inflation-adjusted interest rates on bank deposits were at a level of almost -2.00%. Four years later, the same interest rate was at a level of almost +4.00%.

The return on share prices in Spain shows a similar development compared to Germany. However, the Spanish debt crisis seems to had a distinct negative impact on the stock market. Between 2011 and 2013, the development was marked with a return on share prices on a much lower level compared to Germany. The following table shows the results of the correlation evaluation. The explanatory notes to the evaluation of Germany apply here as well.

	Correlation with MRO lending rate (1999-2016)					
nominal interest rate	Pearson product-moment correlation coefficient	Significance (two-sided)	Kendall rank correlation coefficient	Significance (two-sided)	Spearman's rank correlation coefficient	Significance (two-sided)
Long-term interest rates	0,487	yes (0.1 level)	0,336	yes (0.1 level)	0,443	yes (0.1 level)
Bank interest rates on deposits	0,788	yes (0.1 level)	0,633	yes (0.1 level)	0,783	yes (0.1 level)
Return on share price index	-0,034	no (0,638)	-0,010	no (0,846)	-0,018	no (0,804)
inflation-adjusted interest rate	Pearson product-moment correlation coefficient	Significance (two-sided)	Kendall rank correlation coefficient	Significance (two-sided)	Spearman's rank correlation coefficient	Significance (two-sided)
Long-term interest rates	0,487	yes (0.1 level)	-0,329	yes (0.1 level)	-0,505	yes (0.1 level)
Bank interest rates on deposits	-0,298	yes (0.1 level)	-0,223	yes (0.1 level)	-0,353	yes (0.1 level)

Table 8: Correlation of yield levels in Spain with the MRO lending rate
(Illustration by author, data source: ECB 2016j, Eurostat 2016,
Statistical Data Warehouse of the ECB 2016b, OECD 2016d)

The results show a clear difference compared to Germany. Especially long-term interest rates are obviously less positively correlated to the MRO lending rate. This can be explained by the Spanish debt crisis. Even through decreasing key interest rates and asset purchase programs, the funding pressure and market dynamics prevent a similar proportional falling of interest rates compared to Germany.

The Durbin-Watson test indicates with a value of 0,050 for long-term interest rates and with a value of 0,097 for bank interest rates also a pronounced autocorrelation.

	Correlation with asset purchase programs (2009-2016)					
nominal interest rate	Pearson product-moment correlation coefficient	Significance (two-sided)	Kendall rank correlation coefficient	Significance (two-sided)	Spearman's rank correlation coefficient	Significance (two-sided)
Long-term interest rates	-0,543	yes (0.1 level)	-0,088	no (0,236)	-0,210	yes (0.1 level)
Bank interest rates on deposits	-0,675	yes (0.1 level)	-0,373	yes (0.1 level)	-0,587	yes (0.1 level)
Return on share price index	-0,405	yes (0.1 level)	-0,293	yes (0.1 level)	-0,419	yes (0.1 level)

Table 9: Correlation of yield levels in Spain with asset purchase programs by the ECB
(Illustration by author, data source: ECB 2016j, Eurostat 2016,
Statistical Data Warehouse of the ECB 2016b, OECD 2016d)

Table 9 shows the same phenomenon as described in the context of the correlation of long-term interest rates with the MRO lending rate. Because of funding pressure and market dynamics, the impact of asset purchase programs is limited or at a lower extent effective. This could be a plausible reason for the difference of the correlation compared to long-term interest rates of Germany.

5.4. The Development of Yield Levels in Luxembourg

The following illustration shows the development of the inflation-adjusted interest rates in Luxembourg. The explanatory notes to the diagram of Germany and Spain apply here as well.

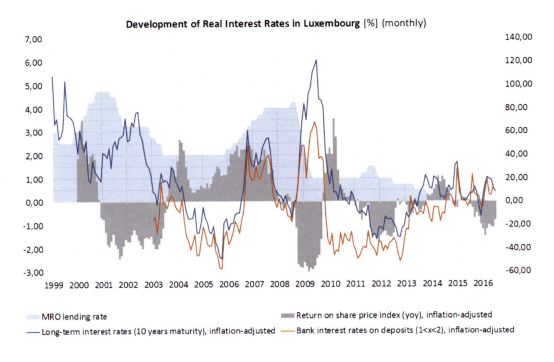

Figure 19: Development of real interest rates in Luxembourg
(Illustration by author, data source: ECB 2016j, Eurostat 2016,
Statistical Data Warehouse of the ECB 2016b, OECD 2016d)

The diagram shows that long-term interest rates and interest rates on bank deposits are similar to Spain in 2016 on a positive level. The diagram shows also that interest rates on deposits were negative between 2010 and 2012, and between 2004 and 2006. Long-term interest rates were negative between 2011 and 2013, and between 2004 and 2006. This development is an analogical development compared to Spain and in sharp contrast to the development of Germany. This could be explained by the similar development of inflation in Luxembourg and Spain between 2004 and 2007, where Germany had a considerably lower level of inflation (see figure 17). According to the illustrations, Luxembourg had the lowest inflation-adjusted interest rates in the past 16 years, related to long-term debt securities as well as bank deposits compared to Spain and Germany. In 2005 the inflation-adjusted long-term interest rate was almost -2,50% and the inflation-adjusted bank interest rate was almost -3,00%.

The following table shows the results of the correlation evaluation. The explanatory notes to the evaluation of Germany and Spain apply here as well.

	Correlation with MRO lending rate (1999-2016)					
nominal interest rate	Pearson product-moment correlation coefficient	Significance (two-sided)	Kendall rank correlation coefficient	Significance (two-sided)	Spearman's rank correlation coefficient	Significance (two-sided)
Long-term interest rates	0,854	yes (0.1 level)	0,709	yes (0.1 level)	0,868	yes (0.1 level)
Bank interest rates on deposits	0,951	yes (0.1 level)	0,821	yes (0.1 level)	0,834	yes (0.1 level)
Return on share price index	0,095	no (0,182**)	0,093	no (0,059**)	0,108	no (0,128**)
inflation-adjusted interest rate	Pearson product-moment correlation coefficient	Significance (two-sided)	Kendall rank correlation coefficient	Significance (two-sided)	Spearman's rank correlation coefficient	Significance (two-sided)
Long-term interest rates	0,307	yes (0.1 level)	0,196	yes (0.1 level)	0,354	yes (0.1 level)
Bank interest rates on deposits	0,157	no (0,045**)	0,008	no (0,879)	0,037	no (0,643)

**0.05 level

Table 10: Correlation of yield levels in Luxembourg with the MRO lending rate
(Illustration by author, data source: ECB 2016j, Eurostat 2016,
Statistical Data Warehouse of the ECB 2016b,
OECD 2016d)

The correlation evaluation shows a strong correlation of nominal interest rates to the MRO lending rate. The strength of correlation is comparable to the strength of the correlation observed in Germany. This indicates again, that there must be a significant factor that reduces the correlation of especially nominal long-term interest rates in Spain. This observation underpins the explanation approach in the evaluation to the Spanish nominal long-term interest rates. The lack of significant correlation of inflation-adjusted interest rates indicates a more volatile inflation development compared to Germany.

The Durbin-Watson test indicates with a value of 0,070 for long-term interest rates a strong and with a value of 0,697 for bank interest rates a significantly lower autocorrelation.

nominal interest rate	Correlation with asset purchase programs (2009-2016)					
	Pearson product-moment correlation coefficient	Significance (two-sided)	Kendall rank correlation coefficient	Significance (two-sided)	Spearman's rank correlation coefficient	Significance (two-sided)
Long-term interest rates	0,730	yes (0.1 level)	-0,610	yes (0.1 level)	-0,809	yes (0.1 level)
Bank interest rates on deposits		yes (0.1 level)	-0,314	yes (0.1 level)	-0,479	yes (0.1 level)
Return on share price index		yes (0.1 level)	-0,386	yes (0.1 level)	-0,505	yes (0.1 level)

Table 11: Correlation of yield levels in Luxembourg with asset purchase programs by the ECB
(Illustration by author, data source: ECB 2016j, Eurostat 2016,
Statistical Data Warehouse of the ECB 2016b,
OECD 2016d)

The correlations of long-term interest rates and bank interest rates to the APPs of Luxembourg have similar characteristics compared to the results of the evaluation of Germany.

5.5. Results of the Empirical Study

The study of the development of yield levels shows impressively the impact of the latest financial crisis between 2008 and 2009 in Germany, Spain, and Luxembourg. However, the investigation also shows that the real interest rates of long-term debt securities and bank deposits are of considerably different developments between 1999 and 2016, while nominal long-term interest rates and bank interest rates of all three countries are falling since 2012 (see Appendix 5). Although the peak levels of the investigated interest rates of all three countries can be found almost simultaneously in 2009, the development before and after 2009 fluctuates considerably. The reason for the common high in 2009 is a veritable collapse of inflation between 2008 and 2010 (see figure 16). Luxembourg has the highest net saving rate and the highest gross financial assets per capita of the analyzed countries (see figure 15). But, as shown in table 12, Luxembourg has the lowest means of the selected yields.

	inflation-adjusted interest rate	Mean	Standard error of the mean	Standard deviation
Germany	Long-term interest rates	1,72	0,10	1,45
Germany	Bank interest rates on deposits	1,19	0,09	1,20
Germany	Return on share price index	3,13	1,64	23,18
	Mean: 2,01			
Spain	Long-term interest rates	1,92	0,09	1,28
Spain	Bank interest rates on deposits	0,23	0,09	1,19
Spain	Return on share price index	0,32	1,47	20,76
	Mean: 0,82			
Luxembourg	Long-term interest rates	0,92	0,12	1,69
Luxembourg	Bank interest rates on deposits	-0,50	0,11	1,37
Luxembourg	Return on share price index	0,11	2,11	29,82
	Mean: 0,18			

Table 12: Means and standard deviation of the evaluated inflation-adjusted interest rates
(Illustration by author, data source: ECB 2016j, Eurostat 2016,
Statistical Data Warehouse of the ECB 2016b, OECD 2016d)

If all three asset classes are considered together, an overall mean for Luxembourg of 0,18 indicates, that this country had the worst development of real interest rates of all three countries. This also applies if only the means of long-term interest rates and bank interest rates on deposits are taken into account without the development of the return on share prices. The values of the standard deviation indicate furthermore a high volatility within the development of the real interest rates of the selected asset classes. Germany is the country with the highest average inflation-adjusted interest rates, even without considering the development of share prices. Spain is the country with the highest mean interest rate on long-term debt securities, which could be reasoned by the Spanish debt crisis since 2009. Figure 18 shows that long-term interest rates are at a considerably higher level especially since 2009. The high values of the correlation coefficients of nominal interest rates with the MRO lending rate essentially confirm theoretical predictions. Especially regarding bank interest rates on deposits, because these interest rates reflect changes in key interest rates most likely.

Although the rank correlation coefficients were used for the assessment, the Person correlation coefficient indicates similar results. However, the Pearson correlation coefficient can only be used under certain preconditions that could not be met at all times. Conclusive significance tests could not be performed for the Person-correlation mainly due to the presence of heteroscedasticity. This issue could be solved through the identification of the disturbance variables and a subsequent transformation of these variables (Hackl 2005, p. 184). A transformation was omitted, because the rank correlation coefficient can calculate similar qualitative results. Above all, the recognition and interpretation of causality plays an important role (Schäfer 2016, pp. 101 ff.). The existence of autocorrelation regarding almost every analyzed asset class furthermore distorts the significance levels. However, the distorted standard errors as a result of autocorrelation could be corrected by using a covariance matrix (Newey-West) (Schneider, Thesling 2015, p. 7).

A key finding of this study is the significant difference of real interest rates of the countries studied. Of great importance is mainly the difference of bank interest rates on deposits, because the difference is supposed to be lower due to the stronger key interest rate dependence. Wealth distribution effects can thereby arise in a monetary union like the euro area, which counteract a desired balance. Even though Germany has experienced between 2011 and 2013 negative real interest rates, this country seems to be the largest beneficiary of the countries studied within 16 years of ECB-policy.

6. Implications and Evaluation

This section describes the risks and opportunities of the current low interest policy and the extended APPs for savers and the ECB, which arise from theoretical considerations. The findings of this study from chapter 5 are put into context and additional results of other current investigations and evaluations are taken into account as well as practical knowledge of other major central banks. Because risks and opportunities apply for both, the savers and the ECB, this subdivision is kept in the line of argumentation.

6.1. Risks

The main risk or fear of savers and the public is a permanently low nominal interest rate environment, where even real interest levels could be in a negative range for a long time (Deutsche Bundesbank 2015a, p. 14). This accompanies with the fear that savings for retirement increasingly lose its value. However, the illustrations of the development of real interest rates of this study indicate a positive trend, especially regarding bank interest rates on deposits for all three countries since 2010. Another common concern is the emergence of price bubbles of certain markets. This concern in particular relates to the real estate market (Deutsche Bundesbank 2015b). Additionally, the risk emerges that borrowers are tempted to make excessive investments and loans by extremely low lending rates whose redemption is only possible at the current low interest levels. The debtor could be overburdened when interest rates rise (DZ Bank 2016, p. 18). The monetary theory implies an impact of low key interest rates and asset purchase programs by the ECB on the exchange rate of the Euro against other major currencies, especially the U.S. Dollar (Schmolke et al. 2016, p. 4). For this reason, travelling through countries, which are bound to the U.S. Dollar can be more expensive. However, redistributive effects of wealth within the euro area can be considered as a major issue. While German long-term debt securities are currently the only ones which are negative among the countries studied, the structure of one of the major APPs of the ECB, the PSPP has to be questioned. German bonds are currently the highest cumulative monthly net purchases within this program of about EUR 237 billion, whereas Spain with EUR 117 billion and Luxembourg with EUR 1,6 billion have a considerably lower amount. Under its current rules, the ECB purchases within their active APPs bonds in proportion to each euro zone country's economy and population, without probably considering the current long-term interest levels sufficiently (Fairless 2016). Fairless (2016) from the Wall Street Journal even raises the question, if the ECB could adapt its purchases towards countries with more debt, such as Italy and Spain, and buy fewer German bonds. However, such a decision would mean high political relevance (ibid.).

The main risk for the ECB can be considered the ineffectiveness of its low interest policy and their APPs. The monetary policy programs, which are implemented by the ECB, based largely on positive practical experiences of other major central banks, such as the FED (Feldstein 2016). Their implications, however, based mainly on theoretical considerations. The first part of this study shows that different opinions about the mechanism of monetary instruments still exist. This is the reason why many critics of the first major purchase program by the FED in 2009 feared a huge rise in inflation as its outcome, which has not occurred until today. The effectiveness of the purchase programs and low interest rates is therefore uncertain to some extent. This is accompanied by the risk that theoretical assumptions can be put into question, such as the acceptance of homo economicus. (Goldschmidt, Nutzinger 2009). A very practical risk is the possibility to suffer losses with the acquired securities. However, this risk is limited since most of the securities are held until maturity (see chapter 3.3). The main risk of loss would be the insolvency of a state, from which securities were bought. One rule of the ECB regarding their APPs states that securities with an interest rate below the deposit facility may not be purchased (Fairless 2016). However, the interest rate on the deposits facility is currently negative, which means that the possibility of losses is given, at least in this context. Another major issue is the risk that the ECB may lose its independence. According to studies regarding the independence of major central banks, the ECB is the central bank with the highest legal independence worldwide (Weber, Forschner 2014, p. 48). But, the expansion of its purchase programs and its mandate in general could expose the ECB to political demands. This issue could endanger its independence (ibid.). In regard to its endangered independence, the risk of loss of trust by the population emerges as well.

6.2. Opportunities

The average household can benefit from the current low interest environment through the availability of low-interest loans. Empirical investigations have found that the permanent lowering of key interest rates by the ECB since 2009 have not led to a significant increase in lending. Only with the implementation of the APPs, the ECB was able to stimulate lending. Studies show that purchase programs and the provision of unlimited liquidity by central banks have a positive impact on bank lending (Bendel 2015, p. 4). But, these investigations show also a significant difference in the intensity of the impact among major central banks. Asset purchases by the FED, for example, had a more positive impact on lending and the real economy (ibid.). People can furthermore participate indirectly through the actions by the ECB, which ease debt-servicing costs in all European countries and reduce the interest rate payments for the governments (Hoffmann, Zemanek 2012, Abstract). Based on the results of this study, it is possible to recommend, that citizen of member states of the euro area should buy government bonds of member states with higher interest rates. Because no German citizen is forced to buy only German government bonds. Citizen of countries with lower interest rates therefore can buy securities of other member states. This would furthermore strengthen the European Community principle and a European consciousness. In doing so the buying country's inflation rate should be considered in the calculation of the real interest rate. If the German inflation rate is assumed in the calculation of an inflation-adjusted interest rate on Spanish long-term debt securities, the outcome is still significant higher in comparison to German long-term debt securities. Lower exchange rates of the Euro in the wake of the current monetary policy of the ECB can increase the ability of European firms to export their products or services. A plenty of empirical studies confirm this assumption (Schneider, Petersen 2014). People of member states of the euro area can participate indirectly from this situation by job preservation and increased turnovers of the companies for which they are working. Another opportunity to profit from the current situation is to omit postponing purchases. Increased consumption would also boost the economy.

The ECB can use the current circumstances to increase its credibility. Some scholars interpreted the ECB actions in the wake of financial market turbulences as "too little, too late" or as a sign of bad news (Dae Woong et al. 2015, Abstract). The differences as shown in chapter 3.2 of this study regarding the transparency of the

ECB's decisions in comparison to other major central banks should be eliminated, or at least adjusted. With a regular publication of minutes after its Governing Council meetings like the FED, the ECB could establish a pronounced trust of the public and finally an increased credibility with respect to its decisions. If the current monetary policy of the ECB works as desired, the ECB could follow the path of the FED to a worldwide more influential central bank. But until today *"[...] its policy is not proving nearly as effective as similar moves did in the United States."* (Feldstein 2016, p. 105).

6.3. Possibilities and Limitations of the ECB

"[...] the impact of the three-year tender was underestimated when I announced it in December, because many people expected the ECB to expand its government bond purchases, the famous "bazooka". Maybe I should have called the tender "Big Bertha" when I announced it, then everyone would have listened." (Draghi 2012). The question that arises in the context of unconventional measures of the ECB is, whether the ECB has already shot its powder and whether it has further weapon to combat the persistent low level of inflation. Theoretically, the ECB has announced with its OMT program all possible scenarios that are conceivable to do "whatever it takes" to preserve the Euro as currency and the financial stability of the euro area.[20] Because with the OMT, the ECB can intervene potentially limitless (Deutsche Bundesbank 2016e). Moreover, additional measures are conceivable. The ECB could further reduce the interest on deposits held with the ECB. Or, more unconventional, the ECB could buy bank debt, debt of other state-owned entities, and in general different assets together, such as gold, stocks or even real estates (Fairless 2016). But whatever the ECB will do, it must be in the context of its mandate. Against this background, the actions performed by the ECB are limited by nature. Especially since the ECB differs in regard to its main objective from other major central banks, as shown in chapter 3.2 of this study. As long as inflation is considered the main source of financial stability from a conventional perspective, the current mandate of the ECB is sufficient. But, recent investigations show evidence that reaching the inflation target does not necessarily mean that the

---

[20] The term "whatever it takes" was used by Mario Draghi during a press conference on July the 26th 2012 to calm the market and to signal the world that the ECB is ready to take further enlarged unconventional measures to a hitherto unexpected extent (Tagesschau 2012).

financial system is stable (Badea 2015, Abstract). In the wake of financial market turbulences, financial stability has become an important objective for authorities. The legal preconditions may have to be adjusted, especially in regard to the current mandate of the ECB. Landmann et al. (2014) furthermore points out, that the conventional view expects from an environment of low interest rates the emergence of capability to overcome lack of investments, stop deflationary developments, and to stimulate economic growth. But apparently, the monetary policy cannot reach these objectives alone. Maybe monetary policy as it is carried out nowadays creates even wrong incentives. From this perspective, Landmann et al. (2014) argues, that other regulatory measures are required and additional investment programs can be supportive (Landmann 2014). This argumentation goes along with the description of monetary policy in chapter 2.4 where it is shown that the ultimate objective of a central bank is usually a matter of legislature. To blame the central bank from a political view for its unconventional measures to reach is objectives is some kind of misguidance. The policy is also needed to set conditions for an economic recovery. This includes, above all, fiscal policy.

7. Conclusion

This study analyzed the development of inflation-adjusted interest rates of Germany, Spain, and Luxembourg. Main result of the empirical study is a considerably different development of inflation-adjusted long-term interest rates with a maturity of 10 years and bank rates on deposits with an agreed maturity of over one and up to two years. These real interest rates are currently positive in Spain and Luxembourg. Long-term interest rates are negative in Germany, while bank interest rates on deposits are positive. The expression of expropriation of savers, as it is used recently by politicians and media is under different aspects inapplicable. This also applies to the results of this study under the assumptions of interest rate developments. In 2014 and 2015 both interest rates were on average positive in Germany. The level of bank interest rates on deposits was in 2015 on a level comparable with 2004 or 2005 and thus prior to the implementation of unconventional monetary policy measures by the ECB. The peak levels of the analyzed interest rates of Germany, Spain, and Luxembourg are almost at the same time in 2009, which is reasoned by a veritable collapse of inflation between 2008 and 2010 in all three countries. The average inflation-adjusted interest rate of 2,01% per annum of long-term debt securities, bank deposits and return on share prices indicates that Germany seems to be the largest beneficiary within 16 years of ECB-policy compared to an average inflation-adjusted interest rate of 0,82 in Spain and 0,18 in Luxembourg. The study furthermore found that the examined nominal interest rates correlate with the MRO lending rate of the ECB and therefore essentially confirm theoretical predictions. But, the future development of real interest rates depends largely on the development of inflation. The current level of inflation is the second lowest after its all-time low in 2009 in all three analyzed countries within the past 16 years. Germany is currently the only country of the three analyzed with a positive inflation rate. This study furthermore shows, that the ECB uses in addition to a low interest policy asset purchase programs, similar to programs conducted in the U.S., to boost the persistent low inflation. The ECB expects to be as successful as the FED has been with its asset purchase programs. This has to be questioned as long as its purpose is different in comparison to the FED (Feldstein 2016). But, there is evidence that the ECB's measures had been effective. A current investigation from the German Institute for Economic Research concludes, that the ECB helped to boost economy. Above all, the ECB also helped to stabilize consumer prices and tackled effectively the risk of sliding into deflation (Rieth 2016, p. 148). The study furthermore concludes that Germany seems to be one of the main beneficiary of the current monetary policy of the ECB, as production and prices rise. Under these aspects, it can additionally be concluded that the predominantly negative evaluation of the monetary policy of the ECB is contrary to the real development (Winkler 2014). A duration of unjustified criticism may undermine the trust in the ECB in general (ibid.). Moreover, it must be questioned by the public to what extant the policy should combat unemployment and has to reduce exorbitant deficits. Because, under legal aspects, the ECB has solely the mandate to guarantee price stability.

Bibliography

Textbooks:

Anderegg, R. (2007): *Grundzüge der Geldtheorie und Geldpolitik (Basic principles of monetary theory and monetary policy [translation by author])*, first edition, Munich: Oldenbourg Wissenschaftsverlag GmbH.

Anderton, A. (2006): *Economics*, 3rd edition, Delhi: Pearson Education.

Arnold, Roger E. (2008): *Economics*, first edition, Mason, USA: South-Western Cengage Learning.

Barbaroux, N. (2013): *Monetary Policy Rule in Theory and Practice: Facing the internal vs external stability dilemma*, first edition, New York: Routledge.

Barrows, D., Smithin, J. (2009): *Fundamentals of Economics for Business*, 2nd edition, Singapore: Caputs Press Inc.

Belke, A., Polleit, Th. (2009): *Monetary Economics in Globalised Financial Markets*, Berlin: Springer Verlag.

Benassy-Quere, A., Coeure B.,& Jacquet P. (2010): *Economic Policy: Theory and Practice*, first edition, New York: Oxford University Press, Inc.

Blanchard, O., Illing, G. (2009): *Makroökonomie (Macroeconomics [translation by author])*, 5th edition, Munich: Pearson Education.

Bofinger, P. (2015): *Grundzüge der Volkswirtschaftslehre: Eine Einführung in die Wissenschaft von Märkten (Basic principles of Economics: An Introduction to the Science of markets [translation by author])*, London: Pearson Studium.

Brown, William S. (1995): *Principles of Economics*, first edition, Eagan, Minnesota: West Publishing Company.

Croushore, D. (2015): *M&B*, 3rd edition, Stamford, USA: Cengage Learning.

Deepashree, Dr. (2016): *Introductory Macroeconomics*, revised edition, New Delhi, India: Saraswati House Pvt. Ltd.

Dobeck, Mark F., Elliott, E. (2007): *Money*, first edition, London: Greenwood Press.

Durlauf, Steven N., Blume, Lawrence E. (2009): *Monetary Economics*, first edition, Basingstoke, Hampshire, England: Palgrave Macmillan.

Duwendag D., Ketterer K. H., Kösters W., Pohl R., Simmert, D. B. (1999): *Geldtheorie und Geldpolitik in Europa (Monetary Theory and Policy in Europe [translation by author])*, 5th edition, Berlin: Springer Verlag.

Dwivedi, D.N. (2010): *Macroeconomics, Theory and Policy*, 3rd edition, New Delhi: Tata McGraw Hill Education Private Limited.

ECB (2016d): *The European Central Bank, the euro system and the European System of Central Banks*, first edition, Frankfurt: European Central Bank.

Faber, D. (2010): *Auswirkungen geldpolitischer Maßnahmen der Europäischen Zentralbank auf Aktien-, Anleihe- und Währungsmärkte – Eine empirische Untersuchung ausgewählter europäischer Märkte (Effects of monetary policy measures of the European Central Bank on equity, bond and currency markets - An empirical study of selected European markets [translation by author])*, first edition, Munich: Herbert Utz Verlag.

Goldschmidt, N., Nutzinger, Hans G. (2009): *Vom homo oeconomicus. zum homo culturalis: Handlung und Verhalten in der Ökonomie (From homo economicus to homo Culturalis: action and behavior in the economy [translation by author])*, Cultural Economics, Volume 8, first edition, Münster: Lit Verlag.

Güida, Juan J. (2009): *Mikroökonomie und Management – Die Grundlagen (Microeconomics and Management - The Basics [translation by author])*, first edition, Stuttgart: W. Kohlhammer GmbH.

Hackl, P. (2005): *Einführung in die Ökonometrie (Introduction into Econometrics [translation by author])*, first edition, Munich: Pearson Studium.

Harmon, C., Oosterbeek, H., Walker, I. (2000): *The Returns to Education - A Review of Evidence, Issues and Deficiencies in the Literature*, first edition, London: Centre for the Economics of Education, London School of Economics and Political Science.

Handa, J. (2002): *Monetary Economics*, first edition, London: Routledge.

Jain, T. R., Khanna, O. P. (2011): *Economics (for BTM - 1)*, edition 2010-11, New Delhi: V.K. Publications.

Kampmann, R., Walter, J. (2013): *Makroökonomie: Wachstum, Beschäftigung, Außenwirtschaft (Macroeconomics: growth, employment, foreign trade [translation by author])*, first edition, Munich: Oldenbourg Verlag.

Keynes, John M. (1936): *The General Theory of Employment, Interest, and Money (Great Minds Series)*, Reprint 1997, Amherst, New York Prometheus Books.

Koenig, Evan F. (2012): *The Taylor Rule – and the Transformation of Monetary Policy*, first edition, Stanford, California, USA: Hoover Institutions Press.

Koerner, Finn M. (2013): *Wechselkurse und globale Ungleichgewichte: Wirtschaftsentwicklung und Stabilität Deutschlands und Chinas in Bretton Woods I und II (Exchange rates and global imbalances: economic development and stability of Germany and China in Bretton Woods I and II [translation by author])*, first edition, Wiesbaden: Springer Gabler.

Kurihara, Kenneth K. (1950): *Monetary Theory and Public Policy*, first edition, New York: Routledge.

Lipsey, Richard G., Harbury C. (1992): *First Principles of Economics*, 2nd edition, New York: Oxford University Press, Inc.

Lloyd, Th. (2006): *Money, Banking and Financial Markets*, first edition, Mason, USA: Thomson South-Western.

Madura, J. (2014): *Financial Markets and Institutions*, 11th edition, Boston, Massachusetts: Cengage Learning.

Mankiw, N. Gregory (2003): *Macroéconomie*, 3rd edition, Louvain-la-Neuve, Belgium: De Boeck.

Mankiw, N. Gregory (2011): *Principles of Microeconomics*, 6th edition, Mason, USA: Cengage Learning.

Mankiw, N. Gregory (2015): *Principles of Microeconomics*, 7th edition, Mason, USA: Cengage Learning.

Mankiw, N. Gregory, Taylor, Mark P. (2006): *Economics*, first edition, London: Thomson Learning.

Mankiw, N. Gregory, Taylor, Mark P. (2011): *Microeconomics*, 2nd edition, Cheriton Boston, USA: Cengage Learning EMEA.

Mehta, B. K. (2000): *Principles of Money and Banking*, first edition, New Delhi: Shri Jainendra Press.

Miles, D., Scott, A., Breedon, F. (2014): *Makroökonomie: globale Wirtschaftszusammenhänge verstehen (Macroeconomics: understand global economic relationships [translation by author])*, first edition, Berlin: Wiley-VCH Verlag.

Mishkin, Frederic S. (2015): *The Economics of Money, Banking and Financial Markets*, 11th edition, Boston, Massachusetts: Addison Wesley.

Montiel, Peter J. (2011): *Macroeconomics in Emerging Markets*, 2nd edition, Cambridge: Cambridge University Press.

Möller, M. (2011): *Online-Kommunikationsverhalten von Multiplikatoren – Persönlichkeitsspezifische Analyse und Steigerung des Innovationsinput über User Generated Content (Online communication behavior of multipliers - personality-specific analysis and increase the innovations input on user generated content [translation by author])*, first edition, Wiesbaden: Gabler Verlag.

Mueller, C. (2015): *Nachhaltige Ökonomie: Ziele, Herausforderungen und Lösungswege (Sustainable economics: goals, challenges and solutions [translation by author])*, first edition, Berlin: Walter de Gruyter.

McEachern, W. A. (2015): *ECON: MACRO4*, 4th edition, Stamford, USA: Cengage Learning.

OpenStax College (2014): *Principles of Economics Volume 2 of 2*, Textbook Equity Edition, Creative Commons: Lulu.com.

Panten, H.-J., Männel, H., Stössel, R., Fischer, G., Trouvain, F.-J., Hüttl, A., Wilsdorf, M., Floitgraf, H. (1975): *Volkswirtschaftslehre (Macroeconomics [translation by author])*, first edition, Wiesbaden: Betriebswirtschaftlicher Verlag Dr. Th. Gabler.

Ryan-Collins, J., Greenham, T., Werner, R., Jackson, A. (2012): *Where Does Money Come From?: A Guide to the UK Monetary and Banking System*, 2nd edition, new economics foundation cc.

Scarth, W. (2016): *Macroeconomics, The Development of Modern Methods for Policy Analysis*, first edition, Moore Park, California, USA: Content Technologies, Inc.

Schäfer, Th. (2016): *Methodenlehre und Statistik – Einführung in Datenerhebung, deskriptive Statistik und Inferenzstatistik (Methodology and Statistics - Introduction to data collection, descriptive statistics and inferential statistics [translation by author])*, first edition, Wiesbaden: Springer Verlag.

Scheller, H. (2004): *The European Central Bank – History, Role and Functions*, first edition, Frankfurt: European Central Bank.

Schmidt, J. (2012*): Sparen – Fluch oder Segen? (Save - Blessing or Curse? [translation by author])*, published in Held, M. et al. (2012): Normative und institutionelle Grundfragen der Ökonomik, Lehren aus der Krise für die Makroökonomik, Band 11 (Normative and institutional basic questions of economics, lessons from the crisis for Macroeconomics, Volume 11 [translation by author]), first edition, pp. 61-83, Marburg: Metropolis-Verlag.

Schmolke, H. (2015): *The Monetary System and the Money Multiplier: The Impact of U.S. FED Bond Purchases on Inflation since 2008*, first edition, CreateSpace Independent Publishing Platform.

Schmolke, H. et al. (2016): *Forex-Devisenhandel: Auswirkungen der US-amerikanischen Arbeitsmarktberichte und FOMC-Sitzungen (Forex Currency Trading: The Impact of the U.S. labor market reports and FOMC meetings [translation by author])*, first edition, Wiesbaden: Springer Gabler.

Springer Fachmedien Wiesbaden (2013): *Kompakt-Lexikon Wirtschaftspolitik: 3.200 Begriffe nachschlagen, verstehen, anwenden (Compact lexicon economic policy: look-up, understand, apply 3,200 terms [translation by author])*, first edition, Wiesbaden: Springer Gabler.

Stobbe, A. (1994): *Volkswirtschaftliches Rechnungswesen (Economic Accounting [translation by author])*, 8th edition, Berlin: Springer Verlag.

Stoerrle, W. (1970): *Der Marktzins in der unternehmerischen Investitionsentscheidung (The market interest in entrepreneurial investment decision [translation by author])*, first edition, Berlin: Duncker & Humblot.

Sawyer, W. Ch., Sprinkle, R. L. (2015): *Applied International Economics*, 4th edition, London: Routledge.

Teall, John L. (2013): *Financial Trading and Investing*, first edition, Oxford: Academic Press.

Wiley (2015): *Wiley Study Guide for 2015 Level II CFA Exam: Complete Set*, first edition, Hoboken, New Jersey: John Wiley & Sons, Inc.

Wildmann, L. (2012): *Wirtschaftspolitik: Module der Volkswirtschaftslehre, Band 3 (Economic Policy: Modules of Economics, Volume 3 [translation by author])*, 2nd edition, Munich: Oldenbourg Verlag.

Journals, Papers:

Dae Woong, K., Ligthart, N., Mody, A. (2015): *The European Central Bank: Building a Shelter in a Storm*, Griswold Center for Economic Policy Studies, Working Paper No. 248, December 2015.

Deutsche Bundesbank (2015a): *Monatsbericht Oktober 2015 (Monthly Report October 2015 [translation by author])*, Deutsche Bundesbank 2015.

DZ Bank (2016): *Auswirkungen der Niedrigzinsphase auf die privaten Haushalte in Deutschland (Impact of low interest rates on private households in Germany [translation by author])*, Research Publication, Special 11.02.2016.

Schneider, R., Petersen A. K. (2014): *Die Risiken einer Euro-Aufwertung (The risks of a euro appreciation [translation by author])*, Allianz Economic Research, Working Paper 170.

Schneider, R., Thesling, P. (2015): *Erhebliche Renditeeffekte der EZB-Staatsanleihekäufe (Significant yield effects of the ECB's government bond purchases [translation by author])*, Allianz Economic Research, Working Paper 186.

Badea, I. R. (2015): *Monetary Policy under the Border between Price Stability and Financial Stability*, Finance: Challenges of the Future 2015, Issue 17, pp. 158-166.

Bank of Scotland 2015: *Sparerkompass Deutschland 2015 (Saver Compass Germany 2015 [translation by author])*, forsa study on behalf of the Bank of Scotland 2015.

Belke, A., Rees, A. (2014): *Globalisation and monetary policy—A FAVAR analysis for the G7 and the eurozone*, North American Journal of Economics & Finance, July 2014, Vol. 29, pp. 306-321.

Bell, S. (2001): *The role of the state and the hierarchy of money*, Cambridge Journal of Economics. March 2001, Vol. 25, Issue 2, pp. 149-163.

Benchimol, J. (2015): *Money in the production function: A new Keynesian DSGE perspective*, Southern Economic Journal, July 2015, Vol. 82, Issue 1, pp. 152-184.

Bendel, D. (2015): *Die Effektivität der EZB-Liquiditätsmaßnahmen zur Steigerung der Kreditgeschäfte im Euroraum – Darstellung der Schätzmethode (The effectiveness of the ECB liquidity measures to increase credit operations in the euro area - presentation of the estimation method [translation by author])*, Institut der deutschen Wirtschaft, Cologne, Methoden und Daten 1/2015.

Bindseil, U., Domnick, C., & Zeuner, J. (2015): *Critique of accommodating central bank policies and the 'expropriation of the saver' - A review*, European Central Bank, Occasional Paper Series, No. 161, May 2015.

Feldstein, M. (2016): *The Fed's Unconventional Monetary Policy*, Foreign Affairs, May/Jun 2016, Vol. 95, Issue 3, pp. 105-115.

Friedman, M. (1974): *Monetary Correction: A Proposal for Escalator Clauses to Reduce the Costs of Ending Inflation*, Institute of Economic Affairs (IEA) Occasional Paper, No. 41. pp. 9-32.

German Council of Economic Experts (2013): *Stabile Architektur für Europa – Handlungsbedarf im Inland, Jahresgutachten 2012/213 (Robust architecture for Europe – Need for domestic action annual report 2012/213 [translation by author])*, Potsdam: Bonifatius GmbH Buch-Druck-Verlag.

Georgsson, M., Vredin, A., Sommar, P. Å. (2015): *The modern central bank's mandate and the discussion following the financial crisis*, Sveriges Riksbank Economic Review 2015, Issue 1, pp. 7-42.

Greeley, B., Levring, P., Rigillo, N., & Bosley, C. (2015): *The Great Negative Rates Experiment*, Bloomberg Businessweek. October 26, 2015, Issue 4448, pp. 15-16.

Heilmann, D., Lansch, R., Rürup, B. (2014): *Sparverhalten der Deutschen Haushalte – Eine neue Sicht (Savings behavior of German households - A new perspective [translation by author])*, Handelsblatt Research Institut, November 2014.

Hennies, M. O. E. (2005): *Überlegungen zur Effizienz geldpolitischer Maßnahmen des Eurosystems in depressiven Konjunkturphasen (Efficiency considerations of monetary policy measures of the Eurosystem in depressive economic cycles [translation by author])*, 13th Scientific Conference on Economic Policy, 2005, Article in book.

Hoffmann, A., Zemanek, H. (2012): *Financial repression and debt liquidation in the USA and the euro area*, Intereconomics November 2012, Vol. 47, Issue 6, pp. 344-351.

Landmann, O., Boysen-Hogrefe, J., Jannsen, N., Fichtner, F., Schrooten, M., Hüther, M. (2014): *Niedrige Zinsen — gesamtwirtschaftliche Ursachen und Folgen (Low interest rates - macroeconomic causes and consequences [translation by author])*, Wirtschaftsdienst, September 2014, Vol. 94, Issue 9, pp. 611-630.

McLeay, M., Amar, R., Ryland, Th. (2014): *Money creation in the modern economy*, Bank of England Quarterly Bulletin, 2014 1st Quarter, Vol. 54, Issue 1, pp. 14-27.

Mishkin, Frederic S. (2007): *Housing and the Monetary Transmission Mechanism*, National Bureau of Economic Research, Cambridge, Massachusetts, Working Paper 13518.

Monticin, A., Peel, D., Vaciago, G. (2011): *The impact of ECB and FED announcements on the Euro interest rates*, Economics Letters, November 2011, Vol. 113, Issue 2, pp. 139-142.

Platt, G. (2015): *Learning To Live With Negative Interest Rates*, Global Finance, March 2015, Vol. 29, Issue 3, pp. 65-65.

Reinhart, Carmen M., Sbrancia, M. Belen (2011): *The Liquidation of Government Debt*, National Bureau of Economic Research (NBER) Working Paper, March 2011.

Rieth, M., Wittenberg, E. (2016): *"Unsere Untersuchung zeigt, dass die Maßnahmen der EZB sehr effektiv waren": Sieben Fragen an Malte Rieth ("Our study shows that the ECB's measures were very effective": Seven Questions to Malte Rieth [translation by author])*, DIW-Wochenbericht, Vol. 83, Issue 8, p. 148.

Romeo, V. (2016): *Do negative interest rates threaten global economy?*, Money Marketing, 2/18/2016, pp. 24-25.

Ruckriegel, K., Goergens, E., Seitz, F. (2006): *Die vier (!) Ebenen der Geldpolitik oder: Warum die Poole'sche Alternative „Zins- versus Geldmengensteuerung" in Wirklichkeit keine ist ((!) The four levels of monetary policy or: Why Poolean Alternative "interest versus money supply" in reality is not [translation by author])*, WiSt – Wirtschaftswissenschaftliches Studium, Issue 12 2006, pp. 698 – 701.

Socher, K. (1971): *Koordination des Einsatzes geld- und finanzpolitischer Instrumente (Coordination of the Use of Monetary and Fiscal Policy Instruments [translation by author])*, Volkswirtschaftliche Schriften, Heft 172 (Economic writings, Number 172 [translation by author]), Berlin: Duncker & Humblot.

Stakić, N. (2014): *The Role and Importance of ECB's Monetary Policy in the Global Economic Crisis*, Megatrend Review 2014, Vol. 11, Issue 1, pp. 41-52.

Weberm Ch., Forschner, B. (2014): *ECB: Independence at risk?*, Intereconomics, Vol. 49, Issue 1, pp. 45-50.

Wheelock, David C. (2010): *Lessons Learned? Comparing the Federal Reserve's Responses to the Crises of 1929-1933 and 2007-2009*, Federal Reserve Bank of St. Louis Review, March/April 2010, Vol. 92, Issue 2, pp. 89-107.

Winkler, A. (2014): *Dauerkritik an der Europäischen Zentralbank - Falsch angewendete Theorie untergräbt Vertrauen in die Geldpolitik (Criticism of the European Central Bank - False applied theory undermines trust in the monetary policy [translation by author])*, Wirtschaftsdienst, July 2014, Vol. 94, Issue 7, pp. 479-786.

Policies, Laws:

EC Directive 94/19/EC of the European Parliament and of the Council of 30 May 1994 on deposit-guarantee schemes, Official Journal L 135, 31/05/1994 P. 0005 – 0014, available at: http://eur-lex.europa.eu/homepage.html [accessed June 10th 2016].

EC Treaty (Maastricht consolidated version): Article 107, Community policies - Title VII: Economic and monetary policy - Chapter 2: Monetary policy, August 31st 1992, available at: http://eur-lex.europa.eu [accessed June 10th 2016].

EC Treaty (Nice consolidated version): Article 2. Part one, Principles, 10th November 1997, available at: http://eur-lex.europa.eu [accessed June 10th 2016].

German Deposit Guarantee Act (Einlagensicherungsgesetz [EinSiG], translation by author), July 3rd 2015, available at: http://www.bmj.bund.de [accessed June 10th 2016].

The Lisbon Treaty: Article 123, Treaty on the Functioning of the European Union & comments Part 3 - Union policies and internal actions, Title VIII - Economic and monetary policy (Articles 119-144), Chapter 1 - Economic policy, 18th December 2007, available at: http://www.lisbon-treaty.org [accessed June 10th 2016].

Internet, Newspaper:

Angloinfo (2016): *Capital Gains Tax in Spain*, available at: https://www.angloinfo.com [accessed June 10th 2016].

Augustin, Th. (2014): *Statistik I für Studierende der Soziologie, des Nebenfachs Statistik, der Medieninformatik und der Cultural Cognitive Linguistics – Formelsammlung (Statistics I for students of sociology, the minor subject Statistics, the media computer science and the Cultural Cognitive Linguistics – formulary [translation by author])*, available at: http://statsoz-neu.userweb.mwn.de [accessed June 10th 2016].

Bank of Japan (2016a): *The Basic Discount Rates and Basic Loan Rates (Previously Indicated as "Official Discount Rates")*, available at: https://www.boj.or.jp [accessed June 10th 2016].

Bankenverband (2016): *Leitzinsen der Bank of Japan (Key interest rates by the Bank of Japan [translation by author])*, available at: https://bankenverband.de [accessed August 11th 2016].

Bernanke, B. (2007): *Globalization and Monetary Policy*, Speech at the Fourth Economic Summit, Stanford Institute for Economic Policy Research, Stanford, California, March 2nd 2007, available at: http://www.federalreserve.gov [accessed June 10th 2016].

Boston University School of Public Health 2016: *Regression Diagnostics*, available at: http://sphweb.bumc.bu.edu [accessed August 11th 2016].

Bundeszentrale für Steuern (2016): *Kapitalertragssteuerentlastung (Capital gains tax relief [translation by author])*, available at: http://www.bzst.de [accessed August 11th 2016].

CMS Forex (2016): Central Banks You Need to Know, Capital Market Services (BVI) Ltd., available at: http://www.cmsfx.com [accessed June 10th 2016].

Deutsche Bundesbank (2015b): *Preisblasen werden wahrscheinlicher (Price bubbles are likely [translation by author])*, available at: https://www.bundesbank.de [accessed June 8th 2016].

Deutsche Bundesbank (2016a): *Zentralbankgeld (Central bank money [translation by author])*, Glossary, Deutsche Bundesbank, available at: https://www.bundesbank.de [accessed June 8th 2016].

Deutsche Bundesbank (2016b): *Zins (Interest [translation by author])*, Glossary, Deutsche Bundesbank, available at: https://www.bundesbank.de [accessed June 8th 2016].

Deutsche Bundesbank (2016c): *Transmissionsmechanismus (Transmission mechanism [translation by author])*, Glossary, Deutsche Bundesbank, available at: https://www.bundesbank.de [accessed June 8th 2016].

Deutsche Bundesbank (2016d): *Kapitel 6: Die Geldpolitik des Eurosystems (The monetary policy of the Eurosystem [translation by author])*, available at: https://www.bundesbank.de [accessed June 8th 2016].

Deutsche Bundesbank (2016e): *Outright-Geschäfte - Abgeschlossene bzw. angekündigte Program (Outright transactions – Completed or announced programmes [stranslation by author])*, available at: https://www.bundesbank.de [accessed June 8th 2016].

Deutsche Bundesbank (2016f): *Outright-Geschäfte – Allgemeine Informationen (Outright transactions – General information [translation by author])*, available at: https://www.bundesbank.de [accessed June 8th 2016].

Deutsche Bundesbank (2016g): *Umlaufsrenditen (Yield on bonds outstanding [translation by author])*, available at: https://www.bundesbank.de [accessed June 8th 2016].

Draghi, M. (2012): *Interview with Mario Draghi, President of the ECB, conducted by Holger Steltzner and Stefan Ruhkamp*, published 24 February 2012, available at: https://www.ecb.europa.eu [accessed June 8th 2016].

ECB (2016a): *ECB announces details of the corporate sector purchase program (CSPP)*, European Central Bank, Directorate General Communications, April 21, 2016, available at: https://www.ecb.europa.eu [accessed June 8th 2016].

ECB (2016b): *The ECB's definition of euro area monetary aggregates*, European Central Bank, Statistics, available at: https://www.ecb.europa.eu [accessed June 8th 2016].

ECB (2016c): *Transmission mechanism of monetary policy*, European Central Bank, available at: https://www.ecb.europa.eu [accessed July 18th 2016].

ECB (2016d): *General Council*, European Central Bank, available at: https://www.ecb.europa.eu [accessed July 18th 2016].

ECB (2016e): *Supervisory Board*, European Central Bank, available at: https://www.ecb.europa.eu [accessed July 18th 2016].

ECB (2016f): *Capital subscription*, available at: https://www.ecb.europa.eu [accessed July 18th 2016].

ECB (2016g): *Asset purchase programmes*, available at: https://www.ecb.europa.eu [accessed July 18th 2016].

ECB (2016h): *Foreign exchange operations*, available at: https://www.ecb.europa.eu [accessed July 18th 2016].

ECB (2016i): *Minimum reserves and liquidity – Data on daily liquidity conditions*, available at: https://www.ecb.europa.eu [accessed July 18th 2016].

ECB (2016j): *Key ECB interest rates*, available at: https://www.ecb.europa.eu [accessed July 18th 2016].

ECB (2016k): *Open market operations*, available at: https://www.ecb.europa.eu [accessed July 18th 2016].

Elbel, G., Preißmann, J. (2012): *Jährliche Neugewichtung des Harmonisierten Verbraucherpreisindex (Annual weighting of the Harmonized Index of Consumer Prices [translation by author])*, Federal Statistical Office of Germany, August 2012, available at: https://www.destatis.de [accessed July 18th 2016].

Eurostat (2016): *HICP (2015=100) – monthly data (annual rate of change)*, available at: http://ec.europa.eu [accessed August 10th 2016].

euro|topics (2009): *Swedish central bank to charge negative interest rate*, Federal Agency for Political Education of Germany, available at: http://archiv.eurotopics.net [accessed June 8th 2016].

Fairless, T. (2016): *European Central Bank Faces Questions Over Which Bonds to Buy*, The Wall Street Journal, available at: http://www.wsj.com [accessed June 8th 2016].

EP Services (2016): *Becoming Resident in Luxembourg*, available at: http://www.epservices.com [accessed June 8th 2016].

FAZ (2016): *Schäuble: Geldpolitik mitverantwortlich für Erfolge der AfD* [Schäuble: Monetary policy jointly responsible for success of AfD], Frankfurter Allgemeine, April 9, 2016 (translation by author), available at: http://www.faz.net [accessed June 8th 2016].

Federal Reserve (2006): *H.6 Money Stock Measures - Discontinuance of M3*, available at: https://www.federalreserve.gov [accessed June 10th 2016].

Federal Reserve (2016a): *What is the money supply? Is it important?*, Board of Governors of the Federal Reserve System, available at: https://www.federalreserve.gov [accessed June 10th 2016].

Federal Reserve (2016b): *Federal Open Market Committee*, available at: https://www.federalreserve.gov [accessed June 10th 2016].

Federal Reserve (2016c): *Federal Open Market Committee - About the FOMC*, available at: https://www.federalreserve.gov [accessed June 10th 2016].

Federal Reserve (2016d): *What are the Federal Reserve's objectives in conducting monetary policy?*, available at: https://www.federalreserve.gov [accessed June 10th 2016].

Federal Reserve Bank of St. Louis (2016a): *MZM Money Stock*, FRED Economic Data, available at: https://fred.stlouisfed.org [accessed June 10th 2016].

Federal Reserve Bank of St. Louis (2016b): *M2 Money Stock, Consumer Price Index for All Urban Consumers: All Items*, FRED Economic Data, available at: https://fred.stlouisfed.org [accessed June 10th 2016].

Federal Reserve Bank of St. Louis (2016c): *Federal Funds Rate (discontinued), Federal Funds Target Rate – Lower Limit, Federal Funds Target Rate – Upper Limit*, FRED Economic Data, available at: https://fred.stlouisfed.org [accessed June 10th 2016].

Feldstein, M. (2016): *The Shortcomings of Quantitative Easing in Europe*, Project Syndicate, available at: https://www.project-syndicate.org [accessed June 10th 2016].

Financial Times (2015): *Definition of expansionary monetary policy*, Financial Times Lexicon, available at: http://lexicon.ft.com [accessed June 10th 2016].

FOCUS-MONEY (2016): *Europäische Zentralbank in der Kritik, Bayerns Finanzminister wettert: "Die deutschen Sparer werden schleichend enteignet"* ["European Central Bank in the critique, Bavaria's Finance Minister Rails: "German savers are expropriated sneakingly.""], FOCUS Online, April 17, 2016 (translation by author), available at: http://www.focus.de [accessed June 8th 2016].

Gabler Economic Lexicon (2016a): *Geldpolitik (Monetary policy [translation by author])*, available at: http://wirtschaftslexikon.gabler.de [accessed June 8th 2016].

Gabler Economic Lexicon (2016b): *Zwecksparen (Purpose saving [translation by author])*, available at: http://wirtschaftslexikon.gabler.de [accessed June 8th 2016].

Global Investor (2016): *ECB cuts rates and boosts QE*, Euromoney Institutional Investor PLC, available at: http://www.globalinvestormagazine.com [accessed June 8th 2016].

Hedtstück, M. (2016): *EZB kauft jetzt auch Unternehmensanleihen (ECB is now also buying corporate bonds [translation by author])*, available at: http://www.finance-magazin.de [accessed June 8th 2016].

Keller, D. (2013): *Analyse von Zusammenhängen: Korrelation (Analysis of relations: Correlation [translation by author])*, available at: http://www.statistik-und-beratung.de [accessed June 8th 2016].

Landeszentrale für politische Bildung Baden-Würtemberg (2016): *Euro-Krise (European debt crisis [translation by author])*, available at: https://www.lpb-bw.de [accessed June 10th 2016].

n-tv (2016): *Press comments: ECB interest rate decision* [Pressestimmen: EZB-Zinsentscheid], n-tv, detail from the Flensburger Tageblatt, March 11, 2016 (translation by author), available at: http://www.n-tv.de [accessed June 8th 2016].

manager magazin (2014): *Leitzins vs. Aktien - keine Angst vor Zinserhöhungen (Key interest rates vs. Shares – No fear of key interest rate rises [translation by author])*, available at: http://www.manager-magazin.de [accessed June 10th 2016].

New York FED (2016): *The Money Supply*, Federal Reserve Bank of New York, available at: https://www.newyorkfed.org [accessed June 10th 2016].

OECD (2016a): *Inflation (CPI) (indicator)*, doi: 10.1787/eee82e6e-en, available at: https://data.oecd.org [accessed July 18th 2016].

OECD (2016b): *Household financial assets*, available at: https://data.oecd.org [accessed July 18th 2016].

OECD (2016c): *General government debt*, https://data.oecd.org [accessed July 18th 2016].

OECD (2016d): *Monthly Monetary and Financial Statistics (MEI) - Share prices*, https://data.oecd.org [accessed July 18th 2016].

OECD (2014): *National Accounts at a Glance 2014*, available at: http://www.oecd-ilibrary.org [accessed July 18th 2016].

Portland State University (2016): *Financial Repression*, available at: http://web.pdx.edu [accessed July 18th 2016].

Smartinvestor 2016: *Vergleich EZB-FED (Comparison ECB-FED [translation by author])*, available at: http://www.smartinvestor.de [accessed July 18th 2016].

Smith G. (2014): *As the FED leaves the QE party, Japan tops up the punchbowl*, Fortune, October 31, 2014, available at: http://fortune.com [accessed June 8th 2016].

Statistical Data Warehouse of the ECB (2016a): *Financial market data, Business, Euro area, Euro, ECB, Key interest rate*, available at: http://sdw.ecb.europa.eu [accessed August 11th 2016].

Statistical Data Warehouse of the ECB (2016b): *HICP - Overall index, Annual rate of change, Eurostat, neither seasonally nor working day adjusted*, available at: http://sdw.ecb.europa.eu [accessed August 11th 2016].

Statistical Data Warehouse of the ECB (2016b): *Financial markets and interest rates*, available at: http://sdw.ecb.europa.eu [accessed August 11th 2016].

SZ (2016): *Mario Draghi has gone too far* [Mario Draghi hat sich verrannt], Sueddeutsche Zeitung, March 11th, 2016 (translation by author), available at: http://www.sueddeutsche.de [accessed June 8th 2016].

Tagesschau (2012): *Drei Wörter, die den Euro retteten (Three words that saved the Euro [translation by author])*, available at: https://www.tagesschau.de [accessed June 8th 2016].

The Economist (2016): *The European Central Bank's deterrent - The legitimacy of the doctrine that calmed panicky markets is challenged*, June 8th, 2013, available at: http://www.economist.com [accessed June 8th 2016].

Western Carolina University (2016): *Durbin-Watson Statistic & Excel*, available at: http://paws.wcu.edu [accessed June 8th 2016].

Appendices

Appendix 1: Raw Data and its Availability

Title: **Long-term interest rate for convergence purposes**
Title Complement: Long-term interest rate for convergence purposes - Unspecified rate type, Debt security issued, 10 years maturity, New business coverage, denominated in Euro - Unspecified counterpart sector

Country	Series Key	Period	Unit	Frequency
Germany	IRS.M.DE.L.L40.CI.0000.EUR.N.Z	January 1999 - July 2016	Percent	Monthly
Spain	IRS.M.ES.L.L40.CI.0000.EUR.N.Z	January 1999 - July 2016	Percent	Monthly
Luxembourg	IRS.M.LU.L.L40.CI.0000.EUR.N.Z	January 1999 - July 2016	Percent	Monthly

Source: http://sdw.ecb.europa.eu/

Title: **LoBank interest rates - deposits from households with an agreed maturity of over one & up to two years (new business)**
Title Complement: Annualised agreed rate (AAR) / Narrowly defined effective rate (NDER), Credit and other institutions (MFI except MMFs and central banks) reporting sector - Deposits with agreed maturity, Over 1 and up to 2 years original maturity, New business coverage, Households and non-profit institutions serving households (S.14 and S.15) sector, denominated in Euro

Country	Series Key	Period	Unit	Frequency
Germany	MIR.M.DE.B.L22.G.R.A.2250.EUR.N	January 2000 - July 2016	Percent	Monthly
Spain	MIR.M.ES.B.L22.G.R.A.2250.EUR.N	January 2000 - July 2016	Percent	Monthly
Luxembourg	MIR.M.LU.B.L22.G.R.A.2250.EUR.N	January 2003 - July 2016	Percent	Monthly

Source: http://sdw.ecb.europa.eu/

Appendix 2:
Information about the Statistical Concept of the Share Price Indices

Data Characteristics

Unit of measure used: Index

Reference period: 2010=100

Source periodicity: monthly data are averages of daily quotations

Germany

Source: Federal Bank of Germany

Sector coverage: DAX30

Key statistical concept: -

Other manipulations: -

Source: http://stats.oecd.org

Luxembourg

Source: Luxembourg Stock Exchange

Sector coverage: The Lux General Index includes all listed Luxembourg shares.

Key statistical concept: Data refer to the LUX General Index. Dividends are excluded.

Other manipulations: The index is calculated daily. It uses the Paasche formula and is weighted by market capitalisation, i.e. the total number of issued shares multiplied by the price of the day. New shares are added to the index on their first listing day, delisted shares are removed on the daya they are delisted. Data are period averages.

Source: http://stats.oecd.org

Spain

Source: Bank of Spain

Sector coverage: The index covers a selected group of shares, taking into account their market capitalisation and their trading volume and frequency. Currently, the shares of more than 100 companies are included, representing some 85% of total market capitalisation. The composition of the securities included in the index is revised annually.

Key statistical concept: The IGBM (General Index of the Bolsa de Madrid) measures changes in the share prices of companies quoted on the Madrid Stock Exchange. Other manipulations: The index is based on daily closing prices on spot transactions. The general index is calculated as the aggregation of the sector indices weighted by the ratio of market capitalization of the sector. The sector indices are computed as the aggregation of the individual indices weighted by the ratio of market capitalization of the share in the sector. Monthly, quarterly and annual figures are averages of daily prices.

Source: http://stats.oecd.org

Appendix 3: Detailed Values and Results of the analyzed Interest Rates

Germany

Date	Long-term interest rates (10 years maturity) [%]	Long-term interest rates (10 years maturity), inflation-adjusted [%]	Long-term interest rates (10 years maturity), inflation and tax-adjusted [%]	Bank interest rates on deposits [%]	Bank interest rates on deposits, inflation-adjusted [%]	Bank interest rates on deposits, inflation and tax-adjusted [%]	Share price index	Return on share price index (yoy) [%]	Return on share price index (yoy), inflation-adjusted [%]	Return on share price index (yoy), inflation and tax-adjusted [%]	Inflation, mountly data (annual rate of change) [%]
Jan-99	3,70	3,39	2,26	-	-	-	107,00	-	-	-	0,30
Feb-99	3,85	3,75	2,57	-	-	-	104,67	-	-	-	0,10
Mar-99	4,04	3,52	2,30	-	-	-	102,60	-	-	-	0,50
Apr-99	3,85	3,03	1,86	-	-	-	106,89	-	-	-	0,80
May-99	4,01	3,60	2,38	-	-	-	107,65	-	-	-	0,40
Jun-99	4,36	3,94	2,62	-	-	-	108,23	-	-	-	0,40
Jul-99	4,68	4,06	2,64	-	-	-	112,44	-	-	-	0,60
Aug-99	4,88	4,05	2,57	-	-	-	107,62	-	-	-	0,80
Sep-99	5,04	4,21	2,68	-	-	-	108,93	-	-	-	0,80
Oct-99	5,29	4,35	2,75	-	-	-	108,67	-	-	-	0,90
Nov-99	5,04	4,10	2,58	-	-	-	116,82	-	-	-	0,90
Dec-99	5,15	3,80	2,25	-	-	-	126,62	-	-	-	1,30
Jan-00	5,54	3,78	2,11	4,61	2,86	1,48	135,93	27,04	24,91	16,80	1,70
Feb-00	5,51	3,95	2,30	4,72	3,17	1,75	149,87	43,18	41,07	28,09	1,50
Mar-00	5,33	3,88	2,27	4,76	3,31	1,88	157,49	53,50	51,38	35,29	1,40
Apr-00	5,22	4,18	2,60	4,89	3,85	2,37	146,03	36,61	35,26	24,20	1,00
May-00	5,38	4,44	2,81	4,94	4,00	2,51	142,71	32,56	31,38	21,54	0,90
Jun-00	5,19	3,84	2,28	5,14	3,79	2,24	142,60	31,76	30,07	20,51	1,30
Jul-00	5,27	4,12	2,53	5,26	4,11	2,53	140,94	25,34	23,98	16,33	1,10
Aug-00	5,21	4,27	2,70	5,38	4,44	2,81	140,35	30,42	29,26	20,06	0,90
Sep-00	5,26	3,70	2,12	5,47	3,91	2,27	137,55	26,28	24,41	16,52	1,50
Oct-00	5,21	3,76	2,19	5,52	4,06	2,40	130,25	19,86	18,20	12,23	1,40
Nov-00	5,15	3,60	2,05	5,48	3,92	2,27	129,03	10,45	8,82	5,68	1,50
Dec-00	4,89	2,63	1,17	5,32	3,05	1,47	121,25	-4,24	-6,30	-5,04	2,20
Jan-01	4,80	3,46	2,01	4,93	3,58	2,10	121,83	-10,37	-11,52	-8,40	1,30
Feb-01	4,78	2,93	1,50	4,84	2,99	1,54	120,65	-19,50	-20,92	-15,08	1,80
Mar-01	4,67	2,82	1,42	4,79	2,94	1,50	111,33	-29,31	-30,56	-21,78	1,80
Apr-01	4,83	2,57	1,13	4,67	2,42	1,02	111,19	-23,86	-25,50	-18,38	2,20
May-01	5,05	2,19	0,69	4,70	1,85	0,45	114,53	-19,75	-21,93	-16,08	2,80
Jun-01	5,00	2,54	1,05	4,63	2,18	0,80	111,97	-21,48	-23,32	-16,92	2,40
Jul-01	5,02	2,66	1,16	4,61	2,26	0,88	107,89	-23,45	-25,17	-18,18	2,30
Aug-01	4,82	2,46	1,03	4,51	2,16	0,82	101,91	-27,39	-29,02	-20,86	2,30
Sep-01	4,81	2,86	1,42	4,27	2,33	1,05	84,37	-38,66	-39,81	-28,24	1,90
Oct-01	4,60	2,95	1,57	3,96	2,32	1,13	87,78	-32,61	-33,67	-23,88	1,60
Nov-01	4,45	3,11	1,77	3,64	2,31	1,21	94,07	-27,09	-28,03	-19,87	1,30
Dec-01	4,74	3,29	1,87	3,70	2,27	1,16	95,83	-20,96	-22,05	-15,75	1,40
Jan-02	4,86	2,70	1,25	3,81	1,67	0,54	97,94	-19,61	-21,26	-15,40	2,10
Feb-02	4,92	2,96	1,49	3,91	1,97	0,80	94,44	-21,72	-23,18	-16,68	1,90
Mar-02	5,16	3,10	1,56	4,07	2,03	0,81	100,55	-9,68	-11,45	-8,56	2,00
Apr-02	5,15	3,60	2,05	4,13	2,59	1,35	98,82	-11,12	-12,44	-9,09	1,50
May-02	5,17	4,03	2,47	4,10	2,97	1,73	94,43	-17,55	-18,45	-13,15	1,10
Jun-02	5,02	4,08	2,57	4,15	3,22	1,97	85,68	-23,48	-24,16	-17,06	0,90
Jul-02	4,87	3,83	2,36	4,10	3,07	1,83	77,81	-27,88	-28,59	-20,18	1,00
Aug-02	4,59	3,45	2,07	3,76	2,63	1,50	71,97	-29,38	-30,15	-21,28	1,10
Sep-02	4,38	3,24	1,92	3,63	2,50	1,41	63,57	-24,65	-25,47	-18,03	1,10
Oct-02	4,46	3,02	1,68	3,39	1,96	0,94	58,73	-33,09	-34,01	-24,06	1,40
Nov-02	4,48	3,24	1,89	3,35	2,12	1,11	63,46	-32,55	-33,35	-23,54	1,20
Dec-02	4,33	3,09	1,79	3,27	2,05	1,06	60,89	-36,47	-37,22	-26,23	1,20
Jan-03	4,18	3,15	1,89	3,06	2,04	1,12	57,85	-40,93	-41,51	-29,15	1,00
Feb-03	3,95	2,72	1,53	2,89	1,67	0,80	52,17	-44,76	-45,42	-31,93	1,20
Mar-03	4,00	2,77	1,56	2,99	1,77	0,87	49,83	-50,44	-51,03	-35,82	1,20
Apr-03	4,15	3,12	1,87	3,01	1,99	1,08	55,48	-43,86	-44,41	-31,17	1,00
May-03	3,82	3,20	2,04	2,69	2,08	1,26	57,41	-39,20	-39,57	-27,68	0,60
Jun-03	3,62	2,59	1,50	2,69	1,67	0,86	61,82	-27,85	-28,56	-20,15	1,00
Jul-03	3,97	2,94	1,74	2,54	1,52	0,76	64,66	-16,90	-17,72	-12,62	1,00
Aug-03	4,13	3,00	1,75	2,59	1,47	0,69	66,99	-6,93	-7,94	-5,85	1,10
Sep-03	4,17	3,04	1,78	2,46	1,35	0,60	68,45	7,68	6,51	4,19	1,10
Oct-03	4,22	3,09	1,81	2,47	1,36	0,61	68,48	16,60	15,33	10,32	1,10
Nov-03	4,35	3,11	1,80	2,52	1,30	0,54	72,58	14,38	13,03	8,69	1,20
Dec-03	4,29	3,16	1,86	2,84	1,72	0,86	75,24	23,58	22,23	15,12	1,10
Jan-04	4,17	2,93	1,68	2,78	1,56	0,72	78,98	36,51	34,89	23,89	1,20

Feb-04	4,11	3,28	2,04	2,41	1,60	0,87	79,16	51,75	50,55	34,89	0,80
Mar-04	3,91	2,78	1,60	2,31	1,20	0,50	76,70	53,92	52,24	35,98	1,10
Apr-04	4,10	2,36	1,13	2,30	0,59	-0,10	78,67	41,79	39,42	26,88	1,70
May-04	4,25	2,01	0,74	2,33	0,13	-0,57	74,91	30,49	27,68	18,58	2,20
Jun-04	4,31	2,37	1,08	2,46	0,55	-0,19	76,80	24,23	21,91	14,66	1,90
Jul-04	4,24	2,30	1,03	2,43	0,52	-0,21	74,93	15,89	13,73	8,97	1,90
Aug-04	4,08	1,84	0,62	2,50	0,29	-0,45	72,46	8,16	5,83	3,40	2,20
Sep-04	4,02	2,18	0,98	2,50	0,69	-0,06	75,17	9,81	7,87	4,93	1,80
Oct-04	3,89	1,65	0,49	2,67	0,46	-0,34	76,24	11,33	8,93	5,55	2,20
Nov-04	3,78	1,65	0,52	2,41	0,30	-0,42	78,84	8,61	6,38	3,81	2,10
Dec-04	3,58	1,35	0,28	2,39	0,19	-0,53	80,92	7,55	5,23	2,98	2,20
Jan-05	3,56	1,93	0,86	2,72	1,10	0,29	81,76	3,52	1,89	0,83	1,60
Feb-05	3,54	1,71	0,65	2,52	0,71	-0,05	83,67	5,69	3,82	2,12	1,80
Mar-05	3,70	1,87	0,76	2,53	0,72	-0,04	83,99	9,50	7,56	4,72	1,80
Apr-05	3,48	1,95	0,91	2,31	0,80	0,10	82,62	5,03	3,47	1,96	1,50
May-05	3,30	1,57	0,58	2,20	0,49	-0,17	82,10	9,59	7,76	4,88	1,70
Jun-05	3,13	1,31	0,37	2,72	0,90	0,09	86,47	12,59	10,60	6,83	1,80
Jul-05	3,20	1,28	0,32	2,22	0,31	-0,35	89,74	19,76	17,52	11,61	1,90
Aug-05	3,23	1,40	0,44	2,37	0,56	-0,15	92,77	28,04	25,78	17,38	1,80
Sep-05	3,07	0,46	-0,45	2,41	-0,19	-0,90	94,19	25,30	22,12	14,60	2,60
Oct-05	3,24	0,72	-0,24	2,72	0,21	-0,59	94,04	23,34	20,34	13,39	2,50
Nov-05	3,45	1,12	0,10	2,77	0,46	-0,37	96,44	22,33	19,58	12,92	2,30
Dec-05	3,34	1,12	0,12	2,73	0,52	-0,30	100,89	24,68	21,99	14,63	2,20
Jan-06	3,32	1,10	0,11	2,81	0,60	-0,24	104,30	27,57	24,82	16,59	2,20
Feb-06	3,47	1,34	0,31	2,72	0,61	-0,21	109,85	31,30	28,60	19,25	2,10
Mar-06	3,64	1,71	0,62	2,84	0,92	0,07	112,20	33,59	31,10	21,04	1,90
Apr-06	3,89	1,65	0,49	3,09	0,87	-0,05	114,78	38,93	35,94	24,32	2,20
May-06	3,96	1,82	0,64	3,14	1,02	0,08	110,71	34,85	32,08	21,67	2,10
Jun-06	3,96	1,82	0,64	3,23	1,11	0,14	102,91	19,02	16,57	10,89	2,10
Jul-06	4,01	1,87	0,67	3,25	1,13	0,16	104,55	16,50	14,11	9,18	2,10
Aug-06	3,88	1,94	0,78	3,40	1,47	0,45	107,52	15,89	13,73	8,97	1,90
Sep-06	3,75	2,72	1,59	3,41	2,39	1,36	110,35	17,16	16,00	10,82	1,00
Oct-06	3,79	2,76	1,62	3,52	2,50	1,43	115,27	22,58	21,37	14,55	1,00
Nov-06	3,71	2,18	1,06	3,54	2,01	0,95	118,94	23,33	21,51	14,50	1,50
Dec-06	3,77	2,34	1,20	3,60	2,17	1,09	121,65	20,58	18,92	12,72	1,40
Jan-07	4,02	2,28	1,08	3,69	1,96	0,85	125,79	20,60	18,59	12,41	1,70
Feb-07	4,05	2,21	1,00	3,89	2,05	0,89	130,36	18,67	16,57	10,97	1,80
Mar-07	3,94	1,90	0,72	3,92	1,88	0,71	126,97	13,16	10,94	7,01	2,00
Apr-07	4,15	2,01	0,77	3,96	1,82	0,64	136,34	18,78	16,33	10,73	2,10
May-07	4,28	2,34	1,05	4,02	2,08	0,88	140,54	26,94	24,57	16,51	1,90
Jun-07	4,56	2,61	1,25	4,19	2,25	0,99	144,55	40,45	37,83	25,73	1,90
Jul-07	4,50	2,45	1,11	4,28	2,24	0,96	145,19	38,87	36,15	24,52	2,00
Aug-07	4,30	2,36	1,07	4,29	2,35	1,06	136,63	27,08	24,71	16,60	1,90
Sep-07	4,22	1,58	0,32	4,29	1,65	0,37	139,62	26,53	23,33	15,44	2,60
Oct-07	4,28	1,64	0,37	4,29	1,65	0,37	145,68	26,38	23,18	15,34	2,60
Nov-07	4,09	0,76	-0,44	4,33	1,00	-0,28	140,56	18,18	14,40	9,03	3,30
Dec-07	4,21	1,08	-0,17	4,45	1,31	-0,01	143,82	18,22	14,67	9,28	3,10
Jan-08	4,03	1,00	-0,19	4,38	1,34	0,04	132,11	5,03	1,97	0,48	3,00
Feb-08	3,95	0,82	-0,34	4,14	1,01	-0,22	124,89	-4,20	-7,08	-5,84	3,10
Mar-08	3,80	0,48	-0,64	4,18	0,85	-0,38	117,81	-7,21	-10,17	-8,05	3,30
Apr-08	4,04	1,40	0,20	4,27	1,63	0,36	122,50	-10,15	-12,43	-9,41	2,60
May-08	4,20	1,07	-0,18	4,37	1,23	-0,06	126,19	-10,21	-12,91	-9,89	3,10
Jun-08	4,52	1,08	-0,25	4,80	1,35	-0,06	119,73	-17,17	-19,89	-14,83	3,40
Jul-08	4,49	0,96	-0,37	4,97	1,42	-0,04	111,79	-23,00	-25,60	-18,83	3,50
Aug-08	4,20	0,97	-0,27	5,00	1,74	0,27	112,96	-17,32	-19,89	-14,77	3,20
Sep-08	4,09	1,06	-0,15	4,98	1,92	0,45	107,40	-23,08	-25,32	-18,49	3,00
Oct-08	3,88	1,25	0,09	4,85	2,19	0,75	85,01	-41,65	-43,13	-30,75	2,60
Nov-08	3,56	2,13	1,06	4,88	3,43	1,96	79,38	-43,53	-44,31	-31,22	1,40
Dec-08	3,05	1,93	1,01	4,44	3,30	1,96	78,09	-45,70	-46,29	-32,50	1,10
Jan-09	3,07	2,05	1,12	4,08	3,05	1,82	76,41	-42,16	-42,73	-30,00	1,00
Feb-09	3,13	2,11	1,16	3,37	2,35	1,33	71,47	-42,77	-43,34	-30,42	1,00
Mar-09	3,02	2,71	1,79	2,97	2,66	1,76	66,37	-43,67	-43,84	-30,56	0,30
Apr-09	3,13	2,41	1,47	2,69	1,98	1,16	75,61	-38,28	-38,70	-27,11	0,70
May-09	3,37	3,47	2,44	2,17	2,27	1,61	79,71	-36,83	-36,77	-25,52	-0,10
Jun-09	3,47	3,47	2,41	2,28	2,28	1,58	80,14	-33,06	-33,06	-22,98	0,00
Jul-09	3,34	4,17	3,15	2,29	3,11	2,41	80,50	-28,00	-27,42	-18,81	-0,80
Aug-09	3,31	3,31	2,30	2,14	2,14	1,49	87,90	-22,19	-22,19	-15,42	0,00
Sep-09	3,26	3,67	2,68	2,02	2,43	1,81	91,53	-14,78	-14,43	-9,91	-0,40
Oct-09	3,21	3,31	2,33	1,97	2,07	1,47	93,35	9,81	9,92	6,92	-0,10
Nov-09	3,22	2,91	1,93	1,92	1,62	1,03	92,52	16,56	16,21	11,18	0,30
Dec-09	3,14	2,12	1,17	1,94	0,93	0,34	95,85	22,74	21,53	14,66	1,00
Jan-10	3,26	2,54	1,55	1,88	1,17	0,60	96,47	26,24	25,36	17,41	0,70
Feb-10	3,17	2,66	1,69	1,87	1,36	0,80	91,80	28,45	27,81	19,17	0,50
Mar-10	3,10	1,78	0,84	1,90	0,59	0,02	97,89	47,49	45,60	31,30	1,30

Apr-10	3,06	2,04	1,12	1,83	0,82	0,27	102,04	34,95	33,61	23,06	1,00
May-10	2,73	1,41	0,59	1,78	0,47	-0,06	95,75	20,13	18,58	12,52	1,30
Jun-10	2,54	1,63	0,86	1,47	0,56	0,12	97,07	21,12	20,04	13,66	0,90
Jul-10	2,62	1,40	0,61	2,06	0,85	0,23	96,91	20,39	18,96	12,82	1,20
Aug-10	2,35	1,34	0,63	2,19	1,18	0,52	97,84	11,31	10,21	6,80	1,00
Sep-10	2,30	0,99	0,29	2,13	0,82	0,18	99,61	8,83	7,43	4,77	1,30
Oct-10	2,35	0,94	0,23	1,89	0,48	-0,09	103,42	10,79	9,26	6,02	1,40
Nov-10	2,53	1,01	0,25	1,74	0,24	-0,29	108,29	17,04	15,31	10,19	1,50
Dec-10	2,91	1,19	0,32	1,84	0,14	-0,41	112,91	17,80	15,83	10,49	1,70
Jan-11	3,02	1,00	0,10	1,95	-0,05	-0,63	113,93	18,10	15,79	10,37	2,00
Feb-11	3,20	0,98	0,02	2,02	-0,18	-0,78	117,36	27,84	25,09	16,78	2,20
Mar-11	3,21	0,89	-0,07	2,14	-0,16	-0,79	112,22	14,64	12,06	7,70	2,30
Apr-11	3,34	0,62	-0,37	2,21	-0,48	-1,13	116,24	13,92	10,93	6,79	2,70
May-11	3,06	0,64	-0,27	2,26	-0,14	-0,81	115,87	21,00	18,17	11,91	2,40
Jun-11	2,89	0,38	-0,48	2,47	-0,03	-0,76	112,67	16,07	13,24	8,46	2,50
Jul-11	2,74	0,04	-0,77	2,39	-0,30	-1,01	114,62	18,27	15,17	9,74	2,70
Aug-11	2,21	-0,38	-1,04	2,39	-0,20	-0,92	93,45	-4,49	-6,91	-5,57	2,60
Sep-11	1,83	-0,94	-1,49	2,31	-0,48	-1,16	85,84	-13,82	-16,17	-12,07	2,80
Oct-11	2,00	-0,78	-1,37	2,17	-0,61	-1,26	92,23	-10,82	-13,25	-10,04	2,80
Nov-11	1,87	-0,90	-1,46	2,08	-0,70	-1,32	91,67	-15,34	-17,65	-13,10	2,80
Dec-11	1,93	-0,36	-0,94	2,11	-0,19	-0,81	92,10	-18,44	-20,27	-14,77	2,30
Jan-12	1,82	-0,47	-1,01	2,18	-0,12	-0,77	98,45	-13,58	-15,53	-11,48	2,30
Feb-12	1,85	-0,63	-1,18	2,20	-0,29	-0,95	106,07	-9,62	-11,83	-8,96	2,50
Mar-12	1,83	-0,46	-1,01	2,14	-0,16	-0,79	108,58	-3,24	-5,41	-4,45	2,30
Apr-12	1,62	-0,66	-1,15	1,97	-0,32	-0,91	105,17	-9,52	-11,56	-8,72	2,30
May-12	1,34	-0,74	-1,14	1,85	-0,24	-0,80	99,25	-14,34	-16,10	-11,82	2,10
Jun-12	1,30	-0,59	-0,98	1,71	-0,19	-0,70	94,56	-16,07	-17,64	-12,83	1,90
Jul-12	1,24	-0,65	-1,02	1,93	0,03	-0,55	99,84	-12,89	-14,52	-10,66	1,90
Aug-12	1,34	-0,84	-1,24	1,92	-0,27	-0,85	105,41	12,79	10,36	6,55	2,20
Sep-12	1,49	-0,60	-1,04	1,79	-0,30	-0,84	109,80	27,91	25,28	16,95	2,10
Oct-12	1,47	-0,52	-0,96	1,72	-0,27	-0,79	110,43	19,73	17,38	11,48	2,00
Nov-12	1,34	-0,55	-0,95	1,78	-0,12	-0,65	110,00	19,99	17,75	11,77	1,90
Dec-12	1,30	-0,69	-1,08	1,59	-0,40	-0,88	115,14	25,02	22,57	15,09	2,00
Jan-13	1,51	-0,38	-0,83	1,57	-0,32	-0,79	117,83	19,68	17,45	11,56	1,90
Feb-13	1,54	-0,26	-0,72	1,26	-0,53	-0,91	117,31	10,60	8,64	5,47	1,80
Mar-13	1,35	-0,44	-0,85	1,21	-0,58	-0,94	120,60	11,07	9,10	5,79	1,80
Apr-13	1,20	0,20	-0,16	1,28	0,28	-0,11	117,70	11,91	10,80	7,21	1,00
May-13	1,29	-0,31	-0,69	1,41	-0,19	-0,61	123,82	24,75	22,79	15,36	1,60
Jun-13	1,53	-0,36	-0,82	1,33	-0,56	-0,96	120,08	26,99	24,62	16,54	1,90
Jul-13	1,56	-0,33	-0,80	1,16	-0,73	-1,07	121,31	21,51	19,24	12,81	1,90
Aug-13	1,73	0,23	-0,29	1,07	-0,42	-0,75	124,32	17,95	16,20	10,81	1,50
Sep-13	1,89	0,38	-0,18	1,11	-0,38	-0,72	126,75	15,43	13,73	9,09	1,50
Oct-13	1,76	0,55	0,02	1,04	-0,16	-0,47	131,21	18,82	17,42	11,74	1,20
Nov-13	1,68	0,08	-0,43	1,04	-0,55	-0,86	136,74	24,31	22,36	15,06	1,60
Dec-13	1,80	0,49	-0,05	0,99	-0,31	-0,60	138,15	19,98	18,44	12,43	1,30
Jan-14	1,76	0,65	0,12	1,00	-0,10	-0,40	141,74	20,29	18,98	12,86	1,10
Feb-14	1,56	0,55	0,08	0,94	-0,06	-0,34	141,58	20,69	19,49	13,25	1,00
Mar-14	1,51	0,70	0,25	0,95	0,15	-0,14	139,23	15,45	14,53	9,86	0,80
Apr-14	1,46	0,26	-0,18	0,99	-0,21	-0,51	140,62	19,47	18,06	12,19	1,20
May-14	1,33	0,63	0,22	0,91	0,21	-0,07	141,67	14,41	13,62	9,25	0,70
Jun-14	1,26	0,36	-0,02	0,97	0,07	-0,22	144,13	20,03	18,96	12,91	0,90
Jul-14	1,11	0,41	0,07	0,86	0,16	-0,10	141,30	16,48	15,67	10,68	0,70
Aug-14	0,95	0,15	-0,14	0,90	0,10	-0,17	134,42	8,12	7,26	4,80	0,80
Sep-14	0,92	0,12	-0,16	0,88	0,08	-0,19	139,11	9,76	8,89	5,93	0,80
Oct-14	0,79	-0,01	-0,25	0,96	0,16	-0,13	130,00	-0,93	-1,71	-1,43	0,80
Nov-14	0,72	0,22	0,00	0,87	0,37	0,10	137,66	0,67	0,17	-0,03	0,50
Dec-14	0,59	0,59	0,41	0,79	0,79	0,55	142,47	3,13	3,13	2,17	0,00
Jan-15	0,39	0,79	0,67	0,87	1,28	1,01	147,20	3,85	4,27	3,09	-0,40
Feb-15	0,30	0,30	0,21	0,71	0,71	0,49	159,26	12,49	12,49	8,68	0,00
Mar-15	0,23	0,03	-0,04	0,81	0,61	0,36	170,25	22,28	22,04	15,25	0,20
Apr-15	0,12	-0,18	-0,22	0,77	0,47	0,23	172,56	22,71	22,34	15,44	0,30
May-15	0,56	-0,04	-0,21	0,74	0,14	-0,09	165,89	17,10	16,40	11,22	0,60
Jun-15	0,79	0,59	0,35	0,70	0,50	0,29	159,73	10,82	10,60	7,31	0,20
Jul-15	0,71	0,61	0,39	0,74	0,64	0,41	160,75	13,76	13,65	9,45	0,10
Aug-15	0,61	0,51	0,32	0,65	0,55	0,35	155,10	15,38	15,27	10,58	0,10
Sep-15	0,65	0,75	0,55	0,87	0,97	0,71	143,86	3,41	3,51	2,47	-0,10
Oct-15	0,52	0,32	0,16	0,71	0,51	0,29	147,37	13,36	13,14	9,07	0,20
Nov-15	0,52	0,32	0,16	0,69	0,49	0,28	157,28	14,25	14,03	9,69	0,20
Dec-15	0,55	0,35	0,18	0,50	0,30	0,15	153,80	7,95	7,74	5,32	0,20
Jan-16	0,43	0,03	-0,10	0,62	0,22	0,03	142,54	-3,17	-3,56	-2,59	0,40
Feb-16	0,17	0,37	0,32	0,71	0,91	0,69	134,38	-15,63	-15,46	-10,68	-0,20
Mar-16	0,17	0,07	0,02	0,82	0,72	0,47	142,28	-16,43	-16,51	-11,51	0,10
Apr-16	0,13	0,43	0,39	0,69	0,99	0,78	144,38	-16,33	-16,07	-11,08	-0,30
May-16	0,13	0,13	0,09	0,69	0,69	0,48	142,48	-14,11	-14,11	-9,81	0,00
Jun-16	-0,02	-0,22	-0,21	0,73	0,53	0,31	139,74	-12,51	-12,69	-8,88	0,20
Jul-16	-0,15	-0,55	-0,50				141,05	-12,25	-12,60	-8,88	0,40

Spain

Date	Long-term interest rates (10 years maturity) [%]	Long-term interest rates (10 years maturity), inflation-adjusted [%]	Long-term interest rates (10 years maturity), inflation and tax-adjusted [%]	Bank interest rates on deposits [%]	Bank interest rates on deposits, inflation-adjusted [%]	Bank interest rates on deposits, inflation and tax-adjusted [%]	Share price index	Return on share price index (yoy) [%]	Return on share price index (yoy), inflation-adjusted [%]	Return on share price index (yoy), inflation and tax-adjusted [%]	Inflation, mountly data (annual rate of change) [%]
Jan-99	3,88	2,45	1,72	-	-	-	81,42	-	-	-	1,40
Feb-99	4,02	2,18	1,43	-	-	-	81,25	-	-	-	1,80
Mar-99	4,26	2,12	1,32	-	-	-	81,78	-	-	-	2,10
Apr-99	4,09	1,75	0,99	-	-	-	82,06	-	-	-	2,30
May-99	4,28	2,14	1,34	-	-	-	83,20	-	-	-	2,10
Jun-99	4,61	2,46	1,60	-	-	-	84,04	-	-	-	2,10
Jul-99	4,91	2,75	1,84	-	-	-	83,09	-	-	-	2,10
Aug-99	5,17	2,81	1,85	-	-	-	79,78	-	-	-	2,30
Sep-99	5,32	2,75	1,77	-	-	-	81,43	-	-	-	2,50
Oct-99	5,56	3,09	2,05	-	-	-	79,28	-	-	-	2,40
Nov-99	5,28	2,51	1,54	-	-	-	86,19	-	-	-	2,70
Dec-99	5,37	2,50	1,51	-	-	-	92,46	-	-	-	2,80
Jan-00	5,76	2,78	1,72	2,97	0,07	-0,48	91,23	12,04	8,88	6,66	2,90
Feb-00	5,73	2,65	1,59	3,04	0,04	-0,52	99,80	22,84	19,26	15,05	3,00
Mar-00	5,55	2,48	1,45	3,21	0,20	-0,39	103,40	26,43	22,75	17,88	3,00
Apr-00	5,45	2,38	1,37	3,24	0,23	-0,36	97,30	18,57	15,12	11,69	3,00
May-00	5,63	2,35	1,32	3,42	0,21	-0,42	93,28	12,12	8,64	6,41	3,20
Jun-00	5,45	1,88	0,88	3,55	0,05	-0,60	91,50	8,88	5,20	3,57	3,50
Jul-00	5,53	1,76	0,75	3,72	0,02	-0,66	92,45	11,26	7,29	5,23	3,70
Aug-00	5,50	1,83	0,83	3,77	0,16	-0,53	93,91	17,72	13,63	10,38	3,60
Sep-00	5,56	1,79	0,77	3,71	0,01	-0,67	95,81	17,66	13,46	10,22	3,70
Oct-00	5,50	1,44	0,44	3,88	-0,12	-0,82	92,31	16,44	11,96	8,96	4,00
Nov-00	5,45	1,30	0,30	4,07	-0,03	-0,77	87,42	1,43	-2,56	-2,82	4,10
Dec-00	5,20	1,15	0,20	3,88	-0,12	-0,82	82,74	-10,51	-13,95	-12,03	4,00
Jan-01	5,08	2,12	1,18	3,78	0,86	0,16	86,76	-4,90	-7,58	-6,67	2,90
Feb-01	5,12	2,36	1,41	3,56	0,84	0,18	86,39	-13,44	-15,72	-13,23	2,70
Mar-01	5,04	1,98	1,05	3,79	0,77	0,07	82,75	-19,96	-22,30	-18,61	3,00
Apr-01	5,18	1,53	0,58	3,64	0,04	-0,63	84,36	-13,30	-16,31	-13,87	3,60
May-01	5,36	1,50	0,52	3,46	-0,33	-0,96	85,64	-8,19	-11,55	-10,05	3,80
Jun-01	5,33	1,57	0,60	3,36	-0,33	-0,94	82,55	-9,78	-13,00	-11,21	3,70
Jul-01	5,35	2,88	1,89	3,38	0,96	0,33	76,49	-17,27	-19,20	-16,00	2,40
Aug-01	5,16	3,00	2,04	3,43	1,30	0,66	76,03	-19,05	-20,71	-17,17	2,10
Sep-01	5,14	2,78	1,82	3,21	0,89	0,29	66,94	-30,13	-31,70	-26,11	2,30
Oct-01	4,91	2,35	1,44	2,95	0,44	-0,11	69,66	-24,54	-26,38	-21,83	2,50
Nov-01	4,76	2,20	1,32	2,67	0,17	-0,33	75,79	-13,30	-15,41	-12,95	2,50
Dec-01	4,97	2,41	1,49	2,70	0,20	-0,31	77,17	-6,73	-9,01	-7,76	2,50
Jan-02	5,05	1,89	0,96	2,70	-0,39	-0,89	74,59	-14,03	-16,61	-14,03	3,10
Feb-02	5,11	1,85	0,91	2,83	-0,36	-0,88	73,26	-15,19	-17,82	-15,02	3,20
Mar-02	5,34	2,07	1,09	2,78	-0,41	-0,92	77,09	-6,84	-9,73	-8,47	3,20
Apr-02	5,34	1,58	0,60	2,96	-0,71	-1,26	76,86	-8,90	-12,15	-10,52	3,70
May-02	5,36	1,60	0,62	3,16	-0,52	-1,10	75,78	-11,51	-14,67	-12,56	3,70
Jun-02	5,23	1,77	0,81	3,22	-0,17	-0,77	69,84	-15,40	-18,18	-15,35	3,40
Jul-02	5,07	1,52	0,59	3,12	-0,37	-0,94	63,87	-16,49	-19,32	-16,29	3,50
Aug-02	4,78	1,04	0,17	2,98	-0,69	-1,24	61,26	-19,43	-22,30	-18,74	3,70
Sep-02	4,57	1,03	0,19	2,82	-0,66	-1,17	58,09	-13,23	-16,16	-13,74	3,50
Oct-02	4,63	0,61	-0,24	2,75	-1,20	-1,70	56,65	-18,69	-21,81	-18,40	4,00
Nov-02	4,60	0,67	-0,17	2,67	-1,18	-1,67	61,46	-18,91	-21,96	-18,50	3,90
Dec-02	4,43	0,41	-0,40	2,54	-1,40	-1,87	61,06	-20,88	-23,93	-20,11	4,00
Jan-03	4,24	0,42	-0,35	2,47	-1,28	-1,73	60,82	-18,47	-21,45	-18,07	3,80
Feb-03	4,01	0,11	-0,63	2,49	-1,36	-1,81	57,68	-21,27	-24,22	-20,33	3,90
Mar-03	4,04	0,33	-0,41	2,20	-1,45	-1,85	57,56	-25,34	-28,00	-23,36	3,70
Apr-03	4,19	0,96	0,19	2,16	-1,01	-1,41	62,10	-19,20	-21,71	-18,17	3,20
May-03	3,88	1,15	0,43	2,09	-0,59	-0,98	62,04	-18,14	-20,29	-16,94	2,70
Jun-03	3,69	0,87	0,18	1,83	-0,94	-1,28	66,18	-5,24	-7,82	-6,85	2,80
Jul-03	4,03	1,10	0,35	1,84	-1,03	-1,37	67,50	5,68	2,70	1,65	2,90
Aug-03	4,19	1,06	0,29	1,91	-1,15	-1,51	69,08	12,78	9,39	7,03	3,10
Sep-03	4,21	1,17	0,40	1,93	-1,04	-1,39	69,40	19,49	16,01	12,41	3,00
Oct-03	4,27	1,53	0,74	1,91	-0,77	-1,12	68,60	21,10	17,91	14,01	2,70
Nov-03	4,40	1,46	0,65	2,00	-0,87	-1,24	70,98	15,49	12,23	9,37	2,90
Dec-03	4,34	1,60	0,79	2,01	-0,67	-1,04	73,45	20,30	17,13	13,38	2,70
Jan-04	4,19	1,85	1,07	2,13	-0,17	-0,56	77,29	27,09	24,23	19,20	2,30
Feb-04	4,15	1,91	1,14	2,02	-0,18	-0,55	79,09	37,11	34,16	27,26	2,20

Mar-04	4,01	1,77	1,03	1,97	-0,23	-0,59	78,24	35,93	33,00	26,32	2,20
Apr-04	4,20	1,46	0,68	2,03	-0,65	-1,03	80,69	29,93	26,52	20,98	2,70
May-04	4,33	0,90	0,10	2,04	-1,32	-1,69	77,33	24,65	20,55	16,02	3,40
Jun-04	4,39	0,86	0,05	2,08	-1,37	-1,75	78,68	18,88	14,86	11,40	3,50
Jul-04	4,28	0,95	0,16	2,09	-1,17	-1,56	78,20	15,85	12,15	9,23	3,30
Aug-04	4,15	0,82	0,06	2,05	-1,21	-1,59	76,15	10,23	6,71	4,83	3,30
Sep-04	4,08	0,85	0,10	2,06	-1,10	-1,48	78,97	13,78	10,25	7,72	3,20
Oct-04	3,97	0,36	-0,37	2,10	-1,45	-1,83	81,47	18,76	14,63	11,19	3,60
Nov-04	3,85	0,34	-0,37	2,19	-1,27	-1,67	84,13	18,53	14,52	11,12	3,50
Dec-04	3,64	0,33	-0,34	2,10	-1,16	-1,55	87,46	19,07	15,27	11,76	3,30
Jan-05	3,59	0,48	-0,19	1,93	-1,13	-1,49	89,36	15,62	12,14	9,26	3,10
Feb-05	3,58	0,27	-0,39	1,93	-1,33	-1,68	93,59	18,33	14,55	11,18	3,30
Mar-05	3,74	0,33	-0,36	1,96	-1,39	-1,75	92,90	18,74	14,83	11,39	3,40
Apr-05	3,53	0,03	-0,62	1,93	-1,52	-1,87	91,74	13,70	9,86	7,34	3,50
May-05	3,36	0,25	-0,37	1,87	-1,19	-1,54	92,98	20,24	16,62	12,89	3,10
Jun-05	3,18	-0,02	-0,60	1,72	-1,43	-1,75	96,56	22,72	18,92	14,74	3,20
Jul-05	3,22	-0,08	-0,67	1,77	-1,48	-1,81	99,76	27,57	23,49	18,42	3,30
Aug-05	3,23	-0,07	-0,66	1,80	-1,45	-1,78	101,07	32,72	28,48	22,47	3,30
Sep-05	3,09	-0,68	-1,25	1,76	-1,97	-2,29	105,28	33,32	28,44	22,34	3,80
Oct-05	3,28	-0,21	-0,81	1,87	-1,57	-1,92	106,06	30,19	25,78	20,24	3,50
Nov-05	3,48	0,08	-0,56	2,06	-1,30	-1,67	105,09	24,92	20,82	16,24	3,40
Dec-05	3,37	-0,32	-0,94	2,01	-1,63	-2,00	106,22	21,45	17,12	13,19	3,70
Jan-06	3,33	-0,83	-1,44	2,17	-1,95	-2,34	109,07	22,06	17,14	13,11	4,20
Feb-06	3,48	-0,60	-1,23	2,35	-1,68	-2,11	114,96	22,84	18,00	13,83	4,10
Mar-06	3,66	-0,23	-0,90	2,41	-1,43	-1,87	118,82	27,90	23,10	18,00	3,90
Apr-06	3,92	0,02	-0,70	2,55	-1,30	-1,77	119,14	29,87	24,99	19,53	3,90
May-06	3,99	-0,11	-0,83	2,53	-1,51	-1,97	117,03	25,86	20,90	16,18	4,10
Jun-06	3,99	-0,01	-0,74	2,47	-1,47	-1,92	112,54	16,56	12,08	9,05	4,00
Jul-06	4,02	0,02	-0,72	2,75	-1,20	-1,70	116,10	16,38	11,90	8,91	4,00
Aug-06	3,89	0,09	-0,63	2,48	-1,27	-1,73	120,66	19,38	15,01	11,46	3,80
Sep-06	3,76	0,84	0,14	2,86	-0,04	-0,57	124,94	18,67	15,33	11,88	2,90
Oct-06	3,81	1,18	0,47	3,08	0,47	-0,10	135,33	27,60	24,37	19,26	2,60
Nov-06	3,75	1,02	0,33	3,12	0,41	-0,17	142,36	35,46	31,90	25,34	2,70
Dec-06	3,82	1,09	0,38	3,01	0,30	-0,26	144,20	35,75	32,18	25,57	2,70
Jan-07	4,07	1,63	0,88	3,36	0,94	0,31	147,52	35,25	32,08	25,54	2,40
Feb-07	4,10	1,66	0,90	3,42	1,00	0,36	152,18	32,37	29,27	23,26	2,40
Mar-07	4,01	1,47	0,73	3,39	0,87	0,24	146,13	22,99	19,99	15,73	2,50
Apr-07	4,21	1,67	0,89	3,37	0,85	0,22	152,68	28,15	25,02	19,81	2,50
May-07	4,34	1,89	1,09	2,92	0,51	-0,03	152,41	30,24	27,18	21,57	2,40
Jun-07	4,62	2,17	1,31	3,26	0,84	0,23	153,13	36,06	32,87	26,18	2,40
Jul-07	4,60	2,25	1,39	3,42	1,09	0,46	152,37	31,24	28,29	22,49	2,30
Aug-07	4,40	2,15	1,33	3,42	1,19	0,56	147,53	22,28	19,64	15,50	2,20
Sep-07	4,36	1,62	0,81	3,55	0,83	0,17	145,47	16,43	13,37	10,33	2,70
Oct-07	4,38	0,75	-0,05	4,18	0,56	-0,21	154,16	13,91	9,95	7,40	3,60
Nov-07	4,25	0,14	-0,63	4,28	0,17	-0,61	157,51	10,64	6,29	4,34	4,10
Dec-07	4,35	0,05	-0,74	3,82	-0,46	-1,16	155,68	7,96	3,51	2,06	4,30
Jan-08	4,18	-0,21	-0,97	4,47	0,07	-0,75	139,06	-5,73	-9,71	-8,66	4,40
Feb-08	4,15	-0,33	-1,09	4,27	-0,22	-1,00	132,67	-12,82	-16,58	-14,24	4,50
Mar-08	4,12	-0,46	-1,21	4,02	-0,55	-1,28	130,98	-10,37	-14,31	-12,43	4,60
Apr-08	4,32	0,12	-0,67	4,29	0,09	-0,70	136,73	-10,45	-14,06	-12,15	4,20
May-08	4,43	-0,26	-1,06	4,40	-0,29	-1,09	138,56	-9,09	-13,17	-11,52	4,70
Jun-08	4,79	-0,29	-1,16	4,48	-0,59	-1,40	126,98	-17,08	-21,10	-18,02	5,10
Jul-08	4,80	-0,47	-1,34	4,52	-0,74	-1,56	116,85	-23,31	-27,17	-22,96	5,30
Aug-08	4,56	-0,32	-1,15	4,75	-0,14	-1,00	115,88	-21,45	-25,12	-21,24	4,90
Sep-08	4,57	-0,03	-0,86	4,84	0,23	-0,65	112,18	-22,88	-26,27	-22,12	4,60
Oct-08	4,47	0,84	0,02	4,83	1,19	0,30	95,95	-37,76	-39,92	-33,00	3,60
Nov-08	4,15	1,71	0,94	4,72	2,27	1,39	87,67	-44,34	-45,65	-37,42	2,40
Dec-08	3,86	2,43	1,70	4,40	2,96	2,13	89,25	-42,67	-43,46	-35,47	1,40
Jan-09	4,15	3,32	2,54	4,04	3,21	2,45	86,97	-37,46	-37,95	-30,89	0,80
Feb-09	4,23	3,51	2,71	3,48	2,76	2,10	79,11	-40,37	-40,78	-33,17	0,70
Mar-09	4,06	4,16	3,39	2,91	3,01	2,46	73,43	-43,94	-43,88	-35,52	-0,10
Apr-09	4,01	4,22	3,46	2,55	2,76	2,27	84,02	-38,55	-38,43	-31,09	-0,20
May-09	4,06	5,01	4,23	2,30	3,23	2,79	88,92	-35,83	-35,25	-28,38	-0,90
Jun-09	4,25	5,30	4,49	2,26	3,29	2,86	91,95	-27,58	-26,85	-21,56	-1,00
Jul-09	4,01	5,38	4,61	2,29	3,64	3,20	96,67	-17,27	-16,18	-12,86	-1,30
Aug-09	3,79	4,52	3,80	2,23	2,95	2,52	106,60	-8,01	-7,36	-5,83	-0,70
Sep-09	3,81	4,75	4,02	2,27	3,20	2,76	112,05	-0,11	0,79	0,81	-0,90
Oct-09	3,78	4,41	3,68	1,99	2,61	2,23	113,46	18,25	18,97	15,48	-0,60
Nov-09	3,79	3,38	2,66	2,31	1,90	1,47	113,91	29,93	29,42	23,75	0,40
Dec-09	3,81	2,88	2,17	2,60	1,68	1,20	114,52	28,31	27,17	21,84	0,90
Jan-10	3,99	3,27	2,51	2,59	1,88	1,39	113,47	30,48	29,57	23,82	0,70
Feb-10	3,98	3,57	2,81	2,36	1,95	1,51	100,81	27,43	26,92	21,73	0,40
Mar-10	3,83	1,10	0,39	2,67	-0,03	-0,52	105,23	43,30	39,53	31,52	2,70

Apr-10	3,90	1,46	0,74	3,07	0,65	0,08	106,04	26,20	23,24	18,38	2,40
May-10	4,08	1,54	0,79	3,18	0,66	0,07	91,63	3,05	0,54	-0,03	2,50
Jun-10	4,56	2,41	1,56	2,08	-0,02	-0,41	90,62	-1,45	-3,48	-3,21	2,10
Jul-10	4,43	2,58	1,76	2,78	0,96	0,44	97,00	0,34	-1,43	-1,49	1,80
Aug-10	4,04	2,40	1,65	2,86	1,24	0,71	99,74	-6,43	-7,91	-6,70	1,60
Sep-10	4,09	1,25	0,50	3,21	0,40	-0,19	101,85	-9,11	-11,58	-9,90	2,80
Oct-10	4,04	1,50	0,75	3,09	0,58	0,00	102,81	-9,39	-11,60	-9,86	2,50
Nov-10	4,69	2,34	1,47	3,14	0,82	0,24	96,22	-15,53	-17,43	-14,54	2,30
Dec-10	5,38	2,41	1,42	3,08	0,17	-0,39	94,59	-17,40	-19,73	-16,52	2,90
Jan-11	5,38	2,31	1,32	2,95	-0,05	-0,59	97,45	-14,12	-16,62	-14,02	3,00
Feb-11	5,26	1,80	0,83	2,98	-0,41	-0,95	103,28	2,46	-0,91	-1,36	3,40
Mar-11	5,25	1,89	0,92	2,80	-0,48	-1,00	100,08	-4,89	-7,93	-7,03	3,30
Apr-11	5,33	1,77	0,79	2,89	-0,59	-1,12	101,25	-4,52	-7,75	-6,92	3,50
May-11	5,32	1,86	0,88	3,15	-0,24	-0,82	98,41	7,39	3,86	2,50	3,40
Jun-11	5,48	2,41	1,40	3,33	0,32	-0,29	95,18	5,04	1,98	1,05	3,00
Jul-11	5,83	2,75	1,67	3,13	0,13	-0,45	92,62	-4,52	-7,30	-6,47	3,00
Aug-11	5,25	2,48	1,51	2,86	0,16	-0,37	80,12	-19,67	-21,78	-18,14	2,70
Sep-11	5,20	2,14	1,18	2,89	-0,11	-0,64	76,98	-24,42	-26,62	-22,11	3,00
Oct-11	5,26	2,19	1,22	3,05	0,05	-0,51	82,49	-19,77	-22,10	-18,46	3,00
Nov-11	6,20	3,21	2,06	2,97	0,07	-0,48	77,05	-19,93	-22,19	-18,51	2,90
Dec-11	5,53	3,16	2,13	3,11	0,79	0,21	78,62	-16,88	-18,75	-15,61	2,30
Jan-12	5,41	3,34	2,34	3,11	1,09	0,51	79,19	-18,73	-20,33	-16,84	2,00
Feb-12	5,11	3,15	2,20	2,86	0,94	0,41	81,35	-21,24	-22,71	-18,75	1,90
Mar-12	5,17	3,31	2,35	2,29	0,48	0,05	77,76	-22,30	-23,67	-19,51	1,80
Apr-12	5,79	3,72	2,64	2,23	0,23	-0,19	68,68	-32,17	-33,50	-27,50	2,00
May-12	6,13	4,15	3,01	1,97	0,07	-0,30	62,53	-36,46	-37,64	-30,85	1,90
Jun-12	6,59	4,71	3,48	1,97	0,17	-0,20	61,99	-34,87	-36,02	-29,51	1,80
Jul-12	6,79	4,49	3,23	2,14	-0,06	-0,46	62,26	-32,78	-34,23	-28,13	2,20
Aug-12	6,58	3,78	2,56	2,24	-0,45	-0,86	67,43	-15,84	-18,05	-15,12	2,70
Sep-12	5,91	2,33	1,24	2,68	-0,79	-1,28	74,17	-3,65	-6,91	-6,24	3,50
Oct-12	5,64	2,07	1,03	2,55	-0,92	-1,39	73,19	-11,27	-14,27	-12,20	3,50
Nov-12	5,69	2,61	1,56	2,51	-0,48	-0,94	72,70	-5,64	-8,39	-7,35	3,00
Dec-12	5,34	2,27	1,29	2,69	-0,30	-0,80	75,58	-3,87	-6,67	-5,96	3,00
Jan-13	5,05	2,19	1,26	2,25	-0,54	-0,95	80,58	1,75	-1,03	-1,35	2,80
Feb-13	5,22	2,25	1,29	2,08	-0,80	-1,18	76,63	-5,80	-8,46	-7,39	2,90
Mar-13	4,92	2,26	1,35	2,08	-0,51	-0,89	78,07	0,39	-2,15	-2,23	2,60
Apr-13	4,59	3,04	2,19	2,10	0,59	0,20	75,42	9,81	8,19	6,35	1,50
May-13	4,25	2,41	1,61	2,08	0,28	-0,11	79,19	26,64	24,40	19,43	1,80
Jun-13	4,67	2,42	1,55	1,83	-0,36	-0,70	75,00	20,98	18,38	14,48	2,20
Jul-13	4,67	2,72	1,85	1,89	-0,01	-0,36	75,16	20,74	18,48	14,62	1,90
Aug-13	4,50	2,85	2,01	1,87	0,27	-0,08	80,81	19,84	17,95	14,24	1,60
Sep-13	4,42	3,90	3,06	1,84	1,33	0,99	83,98	13,22	12,66	10,16	0,50
Oct-13	4,22	4,22	3,42	1,82	1,82	1,47	91,86	25,51	25,51	20,66	0,00
Nov-13	4,10	3,79	3,01	1,70	1,40	1,07	92,01	26,56	26,18	21,15	0,30
Dec-13	4,13	3,82	3,04	1,62	1,32	1,01	90,78	20,12	19,76	15,95	0,30
Jan-14	3,79	3,48	2,76	1,56	1,26	0,96	96,05	19,20	18,85	15,21	0,30
Feb-14	3,56	3,46	2,78	1,47	1,37	1,09	95,24	24,30	24,17	19,56	0,10
Mar-14	3,31	3,52	2,89	1,34	1,54	1,29	95,82	22,74	22,99	18,66	-0,20
Apr-14	3,11	2,80	2,21	1,27	0,97	0,73	98,64	30,80	30,40	24,57	0,30
May-14	2,93	2,72	2,17	1,17	0,97	0,75	100,25	26,60	26,34	21,30	0,20
Jun-14	2,72	2,72	2,20	1,08	1,08	0,87	104,62	39,49	39,49	31,98	0,00
Jul-14	2,68	3,09	2,58	1,05	1,46	1,26	101,95	35,63	36,18	29,38	-0,40
Aug-14	2,41	2,92	2,46	0,99	1,50	1,31	98,84	22,31	22,92	18,66	-0,50
Sep-14	2,20	2,51	2,09	0,95	1,25	1,07	103,14	22,82	23,19	18,84	-0,30
Oct-14	2,12	2,32	1,92	0,88	1,08	0,91	97,05	5,65	5,86	4,78	-0,20
Nov-14	2,07	2,58	2,19	0,74	1,25	1,10	97,56	6,02	6,56	5,41	-0,50
Dec-14	1,78	2,91	2,57	0,75	1,87	1,73	98,22	8,20	9,40	7,82	-1,10
Jan-15	1,54	3,09	2,79	0,74	2,27	2,13	95,74	-0,33	1,19	1,26	-1,50
Feb-15	1,52	2,75	2,46	0,63	1,85	1,73	100,87	5,91	7,19	6,06	-1,20
Mar-15	1,23	2,05	1,81	0,62	1,43	1,31	105,54	10,15	11,04	9,09	-0,80
Apr-15	1,31	2,02	1,77	0,55	1,26	1,15	109,01	10,51	11,29	9,28	-0,70
May-15	1,78	2,09	1,75	0,51	0,81	0,72	106,89	6,62	6,94	5,68	-0,30
Jun-15	2,22	2,22	1,80	0,45	0,45	0,36	104,38	-0,23	-0,23	-0,18	0,00
Jul-15	2,10	2,10	1,70	0,47	0,47	0,38	104,74	2,74	2,74	2,22	0,00
Aug-15	1,96	2,47	2,10	0,46	0,96	0,88	101,08	2,26	2,77	2,34	-0,50
Sep-15	2,03	3,16	2,77	0,49	1,61	1,51	91,60	-11,19	-10,21	-8,06	-1,10
Oct-15	1,73	2,65	2,32	0,45	1,36	1,28	95,30	-1,80	-0,91	-0,57	-0,90
Nov-15	1,72	2,13	1,80	0,43	0,83	0,75	96,65	-0,93	-0,53	-0,35	-0,40
Dec-15	1,69	1,79	1,47	0,48	0,58	0,49	91,60	-6,74	-6,64	-5,36	-0,10
Jan-16	1,72	2,13	1,80	0,40	0,80	0,73	82,79	-13,52	-13,17	-10,59	-0,40
Feb-16	1,72	2,75	2,42	0,38	1,39	1,32	77,38	-23,28	-22,51	-18,04	-1,00
Mar-16	1,54	2,57	2,27	0,35	1,36	1,30	83,16	-21,20	-20,41	-16,34	-1,00
Apr-16	1,53	2,76	2,47	0,31	1,53	1,47	82,77	-24,07	-23,15	-18,52	-1,20
May-16	1,57	2,70	2,40	0,28	1,40	1,34	82,58	-22,74	-21,88	-17,51	-1,10
Jun-16	1,48	2,40	2,12	0,26	1,17	1,12	79,05	-24,27	-23,58	-18,93	-0,90
Jul-16	1,17	1,88	1,66	-	-	-	78,49	-25,06	-24,53	-19,73	-0,70

Luxembourg

Date	Long-term interest rates (10 years maturity) [%]	Long-term interest rates (10 years maturity), inflation-adjusted [%]	Long-term interest rates (10 years maturity), inflation and tax-adjusted [%]	Bank interest rates on deposits [%]	Bank interest rates on deposits, inflation-adjusted [%]	Bank interest rates on deposits, inflation and tax-adjusted [%]	Share price index	Return on share price index (yoy) [%]	Return on share price index (yoy), inflation-adjusted [%]	Return on share price index (yoy), inflation and tax-adjusted [%]	Inflation, mountly data (annual rate of change) [%]
Jan-99	3,91	5,39	4,99	-	-	-	87,17	-	-	-	-1,40
Feb-99	3,93	3,31	2,92	-	-	-	85,09	-	-	-	0,60
Mar-99	4,17	3,55	3,13	-	-	-	85,00	-	-	-	0,60
Apr-99	4,01	2,68	2,28	-	-	-	93,15	-	-	-	1,30
May-99	4,16	2,82	2,41	-	-	-	94,77	-	-	-	1,30
Jun-99	4,37	3,13	2,70	-	-	-	94,90	-	-	-	1,20
Jul-99	4,87	5,19	4,70	-	-	-	97,47	-	-	-	-0,30
Aug-99	5,18	3,73	3,22	-	-	-	95,85	-	-	-	1,40
Sep-99	5,31	3,65	3,13	-	-	-	96,23	-	-	-	1,60
Oct-99	5,54	3,57	3,03	-	-	-	94,06	-	-	-	1,90
Nov-99	5,27	3,41	2,89	-	-	-	102,60	-	-	-	1,80
Dec-99	5,26	2,89	2,38	-	-	-	114,78	-	-	-	2,30
Jan-00	5,65	2,08	1,53	-	-	-	123,61	41,80	37,00	32,97	3,50
Feb-00	5,71	3,03	2,47	-	-	-	140,90	65,59	61,39	55,00	2,60
Mar-00	5,56	2,49	1,95	-	-	-	148,79	75,03	69,94	62,65	3,00
Apr-00	5,42	2,15	1,63	-	-	-	143,65	54,21	49,43	44,18	3,20
May-00	5,60	2,62	2,08	-	-	-	137,07	44,64	40,56	36,22	2,90
Jun-00	5,38	0,94	0,42	-	-	-	131,80	38,88	33,03	29,31	4,40
Jul-00	5,57	0,83	0,30	-	-	-	142,03	45,71	39,17	34,80	4,70
Aug-00	5,49	1,73	1,20	-	-	-	140,56	46,64	41,41	36,91	3,70
Sep-00	5,57	1,31	0,78	-	-	-	136,80	42,15	36,42	32,38	4,20
Oct-00	5,51	1,16	0,63	-	-	-	115,75	23,05	17,98	15,77	4,30
Nov-00	5,57	1,02	0,49	-	-	-	109,59	6,81	2,21	1,56	4,50
Dec-00	5,21	0,87	0,37	-	-	-	102,79	-10,45	-14,14	-13,14	4,30
Jan-01	5,06	2,10	1,61	-	-	-	107,54	-13,00	-15,45	-14,19	2,90
Feb-01	5,08	2,02	1,53	-	-	-	106,37	-24,51	-26,71	-24,33	3,00
Mar-01	4,93	1,87	1,40	-	-	-	96,58	-35,09	-36,98	-33,57	3,00
Apr-01	5,05	2,29	1,80	-	-	-	90,69	-36,87	-38,53	-34,94	2,70
May-01	5,30	1,45	0,93	-	-	-	94,10	-31,35	-33,86	-30,84	3,80
Jun-01	5,15	2,39	1,88	-	-	-	97,31	-26,17	-28,11	-25,56	2,70
Jul-01	5,05	2,59	2,09	-	-	-	91,50	-35,58	-37,09	-33,61	2,40
Aug-01	4,81	2,25	1,78	-	-	-	86,66	-38,34	-39,85	-36,11	2,50
Sep-01	4,67	2,72	2,26	-	-	-	71,19	-47,96	-48,93	-44,22	1,90
Oct-01	4,41	2,77	2,33	-	-	-	63,02	-45,56	-46,42	-41,93	1,60
Nov-01	4,29	2,85	2,43	-	-	-	68,83	-37,19	-38,06	-34,39	1,40
Dec-01	4,51	3,58	3,13	-	-	-	70,16	-31,75	-32,36	-29,21	0,90
Jan-02	4,84	2,58	2,11	-	-	-	72,43	-32,65	-34,10	-30,90	2,20
Feb-02	4,91	2,65	2,17	-	-	-	71,10	-33,16	-34,59	-31,35	2,20
Mar-02	5,16	3,40	2,89	-	-	-	70,28	-27,23	-28,45	-25,77	1,70
Apr-02	5,19	3,23	2,72	-	-	-	70,10	-22,70	-24,14	-21,91	1,90
May-02	5,15	3,80	3,29	-	-	-	68,41	-27,30	-28,23	-25,53	1,30
Jun-02	5,09	3,84	3,34	-	-	-	65,61	-32,58	-33,37	-30,16	1,20
Jul-02	4,87	2,91	2,44	-	-	-	58,58	-35,98	-37,17	-33,64	1,90
Aug-02	4,70	2,65	2,19	-	-	-	52,75	-39,13	-40,33	-36,49	2,00
Sep-02	4,33	2,08	1,66	-	-	-	49,86	-29,96	-31,47	-28,54	2,20
Oct-02	4,11	1,57	1,17	-	-	-	44,91	-28,73	-30,47	-27,67	2,50
Nov-02	4,11	1,47	1,07	-	-	-	48,19	-29,99	-31,76	-28,84	2,60
Dec-02	3,97	1,14	0,75	-	-	-	50,68	-27,76	-29,72	-27,02	2,80
Jan-03	3,62	0,41	0,06	2,39	-0,78	-1,02	47,53	-34,38	-36,41	-33,08	3,20
Feb-03	3,55	0,34	0,00	2,50	-0,68	-0,92	43,81	-38,38	-40,29	-36,57	3,20
Mar-03	3,55	-0,14	-0,49	2,27	-1,38	-1,60	43,44	-38,19	-40,39	-36,71	3,70
Apr-03	3,55	0,63	0,29	2,28	-0,60	-0,82	45,93	-34,48	-36,33	-32,98	2,90
May-03	3,55	1,22	0,87	3,17	0,85	0,54	48,00	-29,83	-31,41	-28,50	2,30
Jun-03	2,85	0,83	0,55	1,95	-0,05	-0,24	51,69	-21,22	-22,76	-20,68	2,00
Jul-03	2,85	0,93	0,65	1,77	-0,13	-0,30	54,16	-7,54	-9,27	-8,53	1,90
Aug-03	3,18	0,86	0,55	2,00	-0,29	-0,49	56,39	6,90	4,50	3,82	2,30
Sep-03	3,22	0,60	0,29	2,66	0,06	-0,20	58,86	18,05	15,06	13,30	2,60
Oct-03	3,20	1,47	1,16	1,96	0,26	0,06	59,61	32,74	30,52	27,30	1,70
Nov-03	3,38	1,35	1,02	2,12	0,12	-0,09	62,14	28,96	26,43	23,59	2,00
Dec-03	3,29	0,87	0,55	2,15	-0,24	-0,45	62,91	24,12	21,21	18,85	2,40
Jan-04	3,01	0,69	0,40	1,93	-0,36	-0,55	65,50	37,81	34,71	31,02	2,30
Feb-04	2,94	0,43	0,14	2,02	-0,47	-0,67	68,73	56,88	53,05	47,51	2,50

Mar-04	2,69	0,68	0,41	2,09	0,09	-0,12	66,96	54,14	51,12	45,81	2,00
Apr-04	2,77	0,07	-0,20	1,87	-0,81	-0,99	68,02	48,10	44,20	39,52	2,70
May-04	3,05	-0,43	-0,73	1,96	-1,49	-1,68	64,41	34,17	29,63	26,33	3,50
Jun-04	3,12	-0,75	-1,05	2,14	-1,69	-1,90	63,78	23,40	18,77	16,52	3,90
Jul-04	3,04	-0,73	-1,03	1,66	-2,06	-2,22	63,20	16,69	12,42	10,81	3,80
Aug-04	2,86	-0,71	-0,99	1,76	-1,78	-1,95	62,82	11,40	7,53	6,43	3,60
Sep-04	2,83	-0,26	-0,54	1,65	-1,41	-1,57	65,42	11,14	7,80	6,72	3,10
Oct-04	2,69	-1,35	-1,61	1,69	-2,32	-2,48	68,64	15,14	10,60	9,15	4,10
Nov-04	2,59	-1,36	-1,60	1,62	-2,29	-2,44	71,36	14,84	10,42	8,99	4,00
Dec-04	2,54	-0,93	-1,17	1,78	-1,66	-1,83	74,10	17,78	13,80	12,08	3,50
Jan-05	2,55	-0,24	-0,49	1,70	-1,07	-1,24	75,51	15,28	12,14	10,65	2,80
Feb-05	2,56	-0,72	-0,96	1,86	-1,39	-1,57	79,16	15,17	11,49	10,02	3,30
Mar-05	2,58	-0,89	-1,14	1,61	-1,83	-1,98	80,16	19,72	15,67	13,76	3,50
Apr-05	2,45	-1,30	-1,54	1,81	-1,92	-2,09	78,83	15,88	11,64	10,11	3,80
May-05	2,28	-1,37	-1,59	1,73	-1,90	-2,07	77,05	19,63	15,36	13,47	3,70
Jun-05	2,12	-1,05	-1,25	1,79	-1,37	-1,54	80,04	25,48	21,59	19,12	3,20
Jul-05	2,17	-1,76	-1,97	1,79	-2,13	-2,30	82,03	29,79	24,80	21,94	4,00
Aug-05	2,25	-1,97	-2,18	1,83	-2,37	-2,54	85,24	35,70	30,10	26,68	4,30
Sep-05	2,20	-2,39	-2,60	1,70	-2,87	-3,03	87,59	33,89	27,88	24,65	4,70
Oct-05	2,42	-2,46	-2,69	1,97	-2,89	-3,07	87,94	28,12	22,02	19,34	5,00
Nov-05	2,65	-0,92	-1,17	1,97	-1,57	-1,76	90,86	27,32	22,89	20,26	3,60
Dec-05	2,74	-0,73	-1,00	2,19	-1,27	-1,48	94,23	27,17	22,87	20,25	3,50
Jan-06	2,82	-1,23	-1,50	2,17	-1,85	-2,06	102,62	35,91	30,55	27,10	4,10
Feb-06	2,82	-0,94	-1,22	2,10	-1,64	-1,84	115,85	46,35	40,99	36,53	3,80
Mar-06	2,82	-0,94	-1,22	2,43	-1,32	-1,55	117,04	46,00	40,65	36,22	3,80
Apr-06	2,82	-0,56	-0,83	2,52	-0,85	-1,09	116,89	48,28	43,41	38,74	3,40
May-06	3,08	-0,50	-0,80	2,54	-1,02	-1,27	117,89	53,00	47,69	42,57	3,60
Jun-06	3,38	-0,50	-0,83	2,47	-1,38	-1,61	114,97	43,64	38,25	34,05	3,90
Jul-06	3,49	0,09	-0,25	2,57	-0,80	-1,05	122,62	49,49	44,58	39,79	3,40
Aug-06	3,58	0,47	0,12	2,69	-0,40	-0,66	127,19	49,21	44,73	39,95	3,10
Sep-06	3,67	1,64	1,28	2,83	0,81	0,54	129,80	48,19	45,29	40,56	2,00
Oct-06	3,67	3,05	2,69	2,99	2,38	2,08	132,89	51,11	50,20	45,12	0,60
Nov-06	3,72	1,89	1,52	3,00	1,18	0,88	136,95	50,73	48,06	43,08	1,80
Dec-06	3,77	1,54	1,17	3,13	0,91	0,60	139,28	47,81	44,63	39,95	2,20
Jan-07	3,83	1,50	1,12	3,27	0,95	0,63	142,25	38,61	35,49	31,72	2,30
Feb-07	3,91	2,07	1,69	3,34	1,51	1,18	152,09	31,29	28,97	25,89	1,80
Mar-07	4,02	1,58	1,19	3,43	1,01	0,67	156,89	34,05	30,91	27,58	2,40
Apr-07	4,26	1,72	1,30	3,51	0,99	0,64	163,78	40,11	36,70	32,78	2,50
May-07	4,63	2,28	1,83	3,61	1,28	0,93	163,43	38,63	35,51	31,74	2,30
Jun-07	4,85	2,49	2,02	3,92	1,58	1,20	170,21	48,05	44,72	40,02	2,30
Jul-07	4,84	2,68	2,21	4,02	1,88	1,49	169,74	38,43	35,58	31,81	2,10
Aug-07	4,68	2,73	2,27	3,92	1,98	1,60	159,93	25,73	23,39	20,86	1,90
Sep-07	4,64	2,09	1,64	4,06	1,52	1,13	166,24	28,07	24,95	22,21	2,50
Oct-07	4,63	0,99	0,55	4,03	0,42	0,03	175,15	31,80	27,22	24,15	3,60
Nov-07	4,56	0,54	0,10	4,01	0,01	-0,38	156,12	13,99	9,61	8,26	4,00
Dec-07	4,68	0,36	-0,08	4,03	-0,26	-0,65	159,10	14,23	9,52	8,16	4,30
Jan-08	4,47	0,26	-0,17	4,32	0,12	-0,30	147,97	4,02	-0,17	-0,56	4,20
Feb-08	4,42	0,21	-0,21	3,86	-0,33	-0,70	154,14	1,35	-2,74	-2,87	4,20
Mar-08	4,37	-0,03	-0,45	4,00	-0,38	-0,77	154,53	-1,51	-5,66	-5,51	4,40
Apr-08	4,55	0,24	-0,20	4,18	-0,12	-0,52	165,63	1,13	-3,04	-3,15	4,30
May-08	4,67	-0,12	-0,57	4,14	-0,63	-1,02	182,44	11,63	6,52	5,41	4,80
Jun-08	4,98	-0,30	-0,78	4,61	-0,66	-1,09	185,37	8,91	3,43	2,58	5,30
Jul-08	5,01	-0,75	-1,22	4,88	-0,87	-1,33	160,15	-5,65	-10,83	-10,29	5,80
Aug-08	4,78	-0,02	-0,48	4,61	-0,18	-0,62	157,87	-1,29	-5,81	-5,69	4,80
Sep-08	4,84	0,04	-0,42	4,74	-0,06	-0,51	134,79	-18,92	-22,63	-20,83	4,80
Oct-08	4,68	0,75	0,30	4,73	0,80	0,34	83,72	-52,20	-54,00	-48,97	3,90
Nov-08	4,35	2,30	1,88	3,85	1,81	1,44	69,78	-55,30	-56,18	-50,75	2,00
Dec-08	4,17	3,45	3,03	3,10	2,38	2,08	68,36	-57,03	-57,33	-51,67	0,70
Jan-09	4,18	4,18	3,76	2,39	2,39	2,15	70,70	-52,22	-52,22	-47,00	0,00
Feb-09	4,33	3,50	3,07	1,82	1,01	0,83	68,92	-55,29	-55,65	-50,16	0,80
Mar-09	4,30	4,61	4,18	1,76	2,07	1,89	61,24	-60,37	-60,25	-54,20	-0,30
Apr-09	4,54	4,85	4,40	2,59	2,90	2,64	70,92	-57,18	-57,05	-51,32	-0,30
May-09	4,59	5,54	5,08	2,19	3,12	2,90	74,73	-59,04	-58,67	-52,71	-0,90
Jun-09	4,74	5,80	5,32	2,37	3,40	3,16	82,26	-55,63	-55,18	-49,56	-1,00
Jul-09	4,46	6,05	5,60	1,54	3,09	2,93	81,41	-49,17	-48,39	-43,40	-1,50
Aug-09	4,15	4,36	3,94	1,63	1,83	1,67	85,46	-45,87	-45,76	-41,16	-0,20
Sep-09	3,94	4,36	3,96	1,51	1,92	1,77	90,70	-32,71	-32,44	-29,15	-0,40
Oct-09	3,85	4,06	3,67	1,57	1,77	1,62	89,53	6,94	7,16	6,46	-0,20
Nov-09	3,87	2,13	1,75	1,18	-0,51	-0,63	88,16	26,33	24,22	21,63	1,70
Dec-09	3,80	1,27	0,90	0,85	-1,61	-1,69	98,51	44,11	40,59	36,29	2,50
Jan-10	3,76	0,74	0,37	1,08	-1,86	-1,97	106,20	50,23	45,85	40,97	3,00
Feb-10	3,69	1,36	1,00	0,89	-1,38	-1,47	99,23	43,99	40,75	36,45	2,30
Mar-10	3,60	0,39	0,04	0,82	-2,31	-2,39	108,24	76,76	71,28	63,84	3,20

Apr-10	3,51	0,40	0,06	0,95	-2,09	-2,18	113,52	60,07	55,26	49,43	3,10
May-10	3,17	0,07	-0,24	0,88	-2,15	-2,24	97,99	31,13	27,19	24,17	3,10
Jun-10	3,01	0,69	0,40	0,95	-1,32	-1,41	93,89	14,14	11,57	10,19	2,30
Jul-10	2,98	0,08	-0,21	0,99	-1,86	-1,95	92,43	13,54	10,34	9,03	2,90
Aug-10	2,65	0,15	-0,11	1,09	-1,38	-1,48	93,40	9,29	6,63	5,72	2,50
Sep-10	2,67	-0,03	-0,29	1,01	-1,65	-1,74	96,36	6,24	3,45	2,84	2,70
Oct-10	2,73	-0,17	-0,43	1,13	-1,72	-1,83	95,78	6,98	3,97	3,29	2,90
Nov-10	2,94	0,43	0,14	1,18	-1,29	-1,40	97,44	10,53	7,83	6,80	2,50
Dec-10	3,32	0,21	-0,11	1,15	-1,89	-2,00	105,51	7,10	3,88	3,19	3,10
Jan-11	3,30	-0,10	-0,42	1,23	-2,10	-2,22	104,74	-1,37	-4,62	-4,48	3,40
Feb-11	3,45	-0,43	-0,77	1,36	-2,44	-2,58	104,37	5,18	1,23	0,73	3,90
Mar-11	3,47	-0,51	-0,84	1,59	-2,32	-2,47	100,08	-7,54	-11,10	-10,37	4,00
Apr-11	3,58	-0,40	-0,75	1,84	-2,08	-2,25	98,89	-12,89	-16,24	-15,00	4,00
May-11	3,29	-0,49	-0,81	1,80	-1,93	-2,10	95,69	-2,35	-5,92	-5,70	3,80
Jun-11	3,15	-0,63	-0,93	1,73	-1,99	-2,16	93,13	-0,80	-4,43	-4,36	3,80
Jul-11	3,03	-0,16	-0,46	1,90	-1,26	-1,44	93,90	1,59	-1,56	-1,71	3,20
Aug-11	2,59	-1,07	-1,32	1,80	-1,83	-2,01	74,81	-19,90	-22,76	-20,84	3,70
Sep-11	2,27	-1,47	-1,69	1,80	-1,93	-2,10	68,23	-29,20	-31,79	-28,98	3,80
Oct-11	2,37	-1,38	-1,61	1,65	-2,07	-2,23	72,05	-24,78	-27,53	-25,14	3,80
Nov-11	2,31	-1,63	-1,85	1,56	-2,35	-2,50	71,39	-26,74	-29,55	-26,98	4,00
Dec-11	2,27	-1,09	-1,31	1,66	-1,68	-1,84	71,69	-32,06	-34,29	-31,19	3,40
Jan-12	2,07	-1,09	-1,30	1,38	-1,76	-1,90	76,29	-27,17	-29,43	-26,79	3,20
Feb-12	2,03	-1,23	-1,43	1,09	-2,14	-2,24	78,71	-24,59	-27,00	-24,62	3,30
Mar-12	2,22	-0,66	-0,88	0,95	-1,90	-1,99	76,69	-23,36	-25,52	-23,25	2,90
Apr-12	2,22	-0,76	-0,97	0,86	-2,08	-2,16	71,95	-27,24	-29,36	-26,72	3,00
May-12	1,92	-0,76	-0,95	0,88	-1,77	-1,86	68,10	-28,83	-30,70	-27,89	2,70
Jun-12	1,82	-0,76	-0,94	0,85	-1,71	-1,79	66,23	-28,88	-30,69	-27,87	2,60
Jul-12	1,70	-0,97	-1,14	1,09	-1,57	-1,67	70,05	-25,40	-27,36	-24,89	2,70
Aug-12	1,66	-1,11	-1,27	1,00	-1,75	-1,85	72,06	-3,67	-6,30	-5,94	2,80
Sep-12	1,65	-1,50	-1,66	0,91	-2,22	-2,31	71,83	5,28	2,02	1,50	3,20
Oct-12	1,62	-1,53	-1,69	0,56	-2,56	-2,61	71,66	-0,53	-3,62	-3,57	3,20
Nov-12	1,52	-1,15	-1,30	0,33	-2,31	-2,34	72,31	1,29	-1,37	-1,50	2,70
Dec-12	1,43	-1,04	-1,18	0,80	-1,66	-1,74	74,07	3,33	0,81	0,48	2,50
Jan-13	1,60	-0,49	-0,65	0,80	-1,18	-1,74	75,20	-1,42	-3,45	-3,31	2,10
Feb-13	1,69	-0,69	-0,86	1,16	-1,21	-1,32	72,38	-8,04	-10,19	-9,41	2,40
Mar-13	1,55	-0,44	-0,59	2,20	0,20	-0,02	68,47	-10,72	-12,47	-11,42	2,00
Apr-13	1,41	-0,29	-0,42	1,44	-0,26	-0,40	65,21	-9,36	-10,88	-9,96	1,70
May-13	1,47	0,07	-0,08	1,09	-0,31	-0,41	66,68	-2,09	-3,44	-3,24	1,40
Jun-13	1,76	-0,24	-0,41	1,39	-0,60	-0,73	64,21	-3,05	-4,95	-4,66	2,00
Jul-13	2,02	0,22	0,02	1,31	-0,48	-0,61	65,30	-6,78	-8,43	-7,76	1,80
Aug-13	2,20	0,49	0,28	1,26	-0,43	-0,56	67,73	-6,02	-7,59	-6,99	1,70
Sep-13	2,27	0,66	0,44	1,04	-0,55	-0,65	69,85	-2,76	-4,29	-4,02	1,60
Oct-13	2,14	1,13	0,92	0,98	-0,02	-0,12	72,27	0,85	-0,14	-0,23	1,00
Nov-13	2,01	0,90	0,70	0,82	-0,28	-0,36	77,51	7,20	6,03	5,32	1,10
Dec-13	2,10	0,59	0,38	0,74	-0,75	-0,82	78,55	6,05	4,48	3,88	1,50
Jan-14	2,06	0,55	0,35	0,59	-0,90	-0,95	81,06	7,79	6,19	5,43	1,50
Feb-14	1,87	1,06	0,88	0,57	-0,23	-0,28	80,50	11,21	10,33	9,21	0,80
Mar-14	1,80	0,99	0,81	0,52	-0,28	-0,33	78,99	15,36	14,44	12,92	0,80
Apr-14	1,71	0,80	0,63	0,66	-0,24	-0,30	80,00	22,67	21,58	19,33	0,90
May-14	1,57	0,17	0,01	0,53	-0,86	-0,91	79,00	18,49	16,85	15,03	1,40
Jun-14	1,44	0,24	0,09	0,69	-0,50	-0,57	79,18	23,31	21,85	19,54	1,20
Jul-14	1,26	0,06	-0,07	0,65	-0,54	-0,61	78,43	20,11	18,69	16,70	1,20
Aug-14	1,08	0,38	0,27	0,85	0,15	0,06	76,25	12,58	11,80	10,55	0,70
Sep-14	0,98	0,68	0,58	0,60	0,30	0,24	77,14	10,43	10,10	9,06	0,30
Oct-14	0,87	0,47	0,38	0,66	0,26	0,19	72,63	0,50	0,10	0,05	0,40
Nov-14	0,75	0,55	0,47	0,22	0,02	0,00	74,90	-3,38	-3,57	-3,23	0,20
Dec-14	0,65	1,56	1,50	0,22	-0,28	0,00	75,18	-4,30	-3,43	-2,99	-0,90
Jan-15	0,47	1,69	1,64	0,20	1,42	1,40	75,39	-6,99	-5,86	-5,16	-1,20
Feb-15	0,40	0,70	0,66	0,10	0,40	0,39	80,03	-0,58	-0,28	-0,22	-0,30
Mar-15	0,16	0,06	0,04	0,20	0,10	0,08	82,45	4,38	4,28	3,84	0,10
Apr-15	0,06	0,06	0,05	0,20	0,10	0,08	82,72	3,40	3,40	3,06	0,00
May-15	0,42	0,02	-0,02	0,20	0,10	0,08	81,48	3,14	2,73	2,42	0,40
Jun-15	0,65	0,15	0,08	0,28	-0,22	-0,25	80,25	1,35	0,85	0,71	0,50
Jul-15	0,56	0,36	0,30	0,22	0,02	0,00	76,21	-2,84	-3,03	-2,75	0,20
Aug-15	0,45	0,35	0,30	1,25	1,15	1,02	71,94	-5,65	-5,75	-5,18	0,10
Sep-15	0,43	0,63	0,59	0,12	0,32	0,31	65,96	-14,49	-14,32	-12,86	-0,20
Oct-15	0,31	0,41	0,38	0,12	0,22	0,31	65,55	-9,75	-9,66	-8,68	-0,10
Nov-15	0,25	-0,15	-0,17	0,12	0,22	0,31	65,11	-13,07	-13,41	-12,11	0,40
Dec-15	0,27	-0,62	-0,65	0,69	-0,21	-0,28	60,97	-18,90	-19,62	-17,75	0,90
Jan-16	0,72	0,22	0,15	0,25	-0,25	-0,27	57,34	-23,94	-24,32	-21,94	0,50
Feb-16	0,43	0,73	0,69	0,14	0,44	0,43	55,88	-30,18	-29,97	-26,94	-0,30
Mar-16	0,42	1,03	0,98	0,37	0,98	0,94	62,58	-24,11	-23,65	-21,22	-0,60
Apr-16	0,34	0,95	0,91	0,37	0,27	0,94	65,41	-20,93	-20,45	-18,35	0,60
May-16	0,33	0,94	0,90	0,37	0,27	0,94	63,08	-22,59	-22,12	-19,85	-0,60
Jun-16	0,17	0,57	0,56	0,29	0,69	0,66	61,93	-22,83	-22,52	-20,23	-0,40
Jul-16	0,00	0,40	0,40				63,68	-16,44	-16,11	-14,46	-0,40

Appendix 4: Results and Preconditions of the Correlation Evaluation

Correlation evaluation of nominal interest rates, Germany

Long-term interest rates:

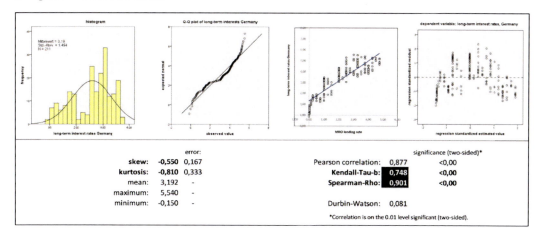

	error:			significance (two-sided)*
skew:	-0,550	0,167	Pearson correlation: 0,877	<0,00
kurtosis:	-0,810	0,333	Kendall-Tau-b: 0,748	<0,00
mean:	3,192	-	Spearman-Rho: 0,901	<0,00
maximum:	5,540	-		
minimum:	-0,150	-	Durbin-Watson: 0,081	

*Correlation is on the 0.01 level significant (two-sided).

Bank interest rates on deposits:

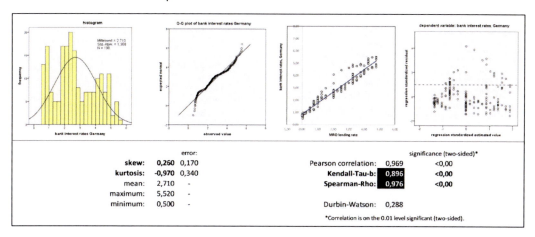

	error:			significance (two-sided)*
skew:	0,260	0,170	Pearson correlation: 0,969	<0,00
kurtosis:	-0,970	0,340	Kendall-Tau-b: 0,896	<0,00
mean:	2,710	-	Spearman-Rho: 0,976	<0,00
maximum:	5,520	-		
minimum:	0,500	-	Durbin-Watson: 0,288	

*Correlation is on the 0.01 level significant (two-sided).

Return on share price index:

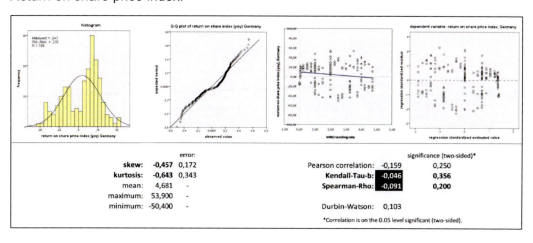

	error:			significance (two-sided)*
skew:	-0,457	0,172	Pearson correlation: -0,159	0,250
kurtosis:	-0,643	0,343	Kendall-Tau-b: -0,046	0,356
mean:	4,681	-	Spearman-Rho: -0,091	0,200
maximum:	53,900	-		
minimum:	-50,400	-	Durbin-Watson: 0,103	

*Correlation is on the 0.05 level significant (two-sided).

Correlation evaluation of inflation-adjusted interest rates, Germany

Long-term interest rates:

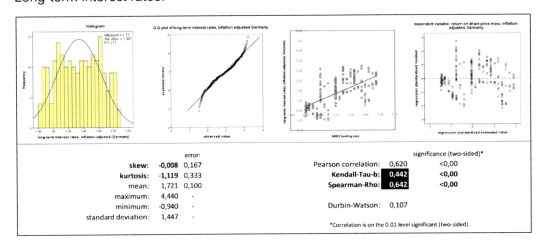

Bank interest rates on deposits

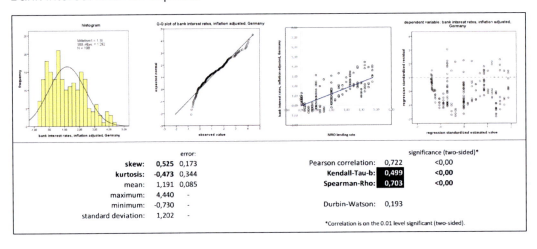

Correlation evaluation of nominal interest rates, Spain

Long-term interest rates:

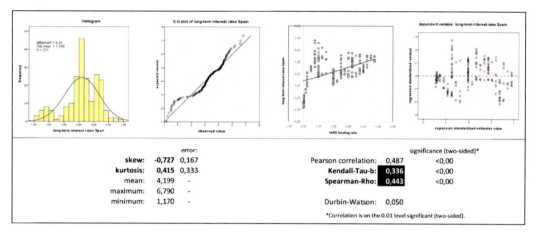

		error:		significance (two-sided)*
skew:	-0,727	0,167	Pearson correlation: 0,487	<0,00
kurtosis:	0,415	0,333	Kendall-Tau-b: 0,336	<0,00
mean:	4,199	-	Spearman-Rho: 0,443	<0,00
maximum:	6,790	-		
minimum:	1,170	-	Durbin-Watson: 0,050	

*Correlation is on the 0.01 level significant (two-sided).

Bank interest rates on deposits:

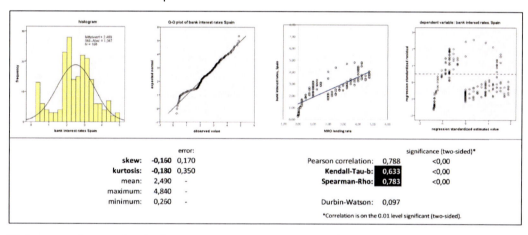

		error:		significance (two-sided)*
skew:	-0,160	0,170	Pearson correlation: 0,788	<0,00
kurtosis:	-0,180	0,350	Kendall-Tau-b: 0,633	<0,00
mean:	2,490	-	Spearman-Rho: 0,783	<0,00
maximum:	4,840	-		
minimum:	0,260	-	Durbin-Watson: 0,097	

*Correlation is on the 0.01 level significant (two-sided).

Return on share price index:

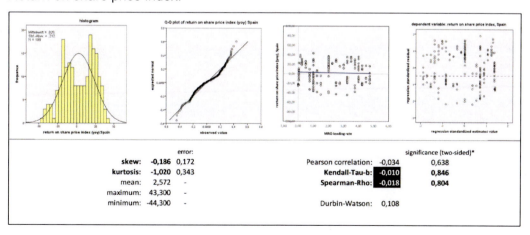

		error:		significance (two-sided)*
skew:	-0,186	0,172	Pearson correlation: -0,034	0,638
kurtosis:	-1,020	0,343	Kendall-Tau-b: -0,010	0,846
mean:	2,572	-	Spearman-Rho: -0,018	0,804
maximum:	43,300	-		
minimum:	-44,300	-	Durbin-Watson: 0,108	

Correlation evaluation of inflation-adjusted interest rates, Spain

Long-term interest rates:

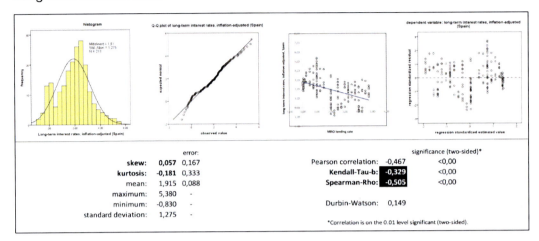

Bank interest rates on deposits:

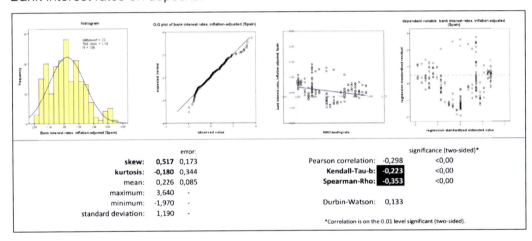

Correlation evaluation of nominal interest rates, Luxembourg

Long-term interest rates:

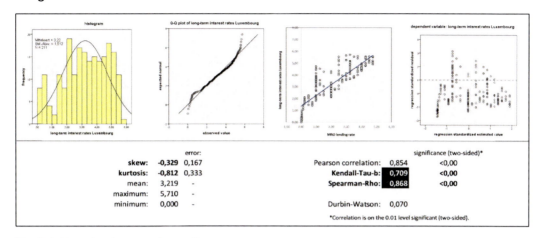

Bank interest rates on deposits:

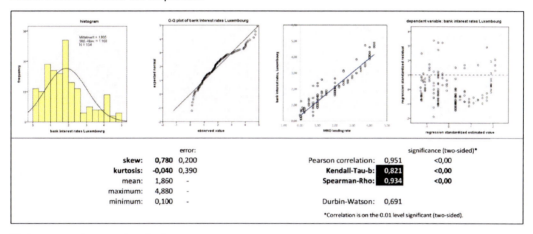

Return on share price index:

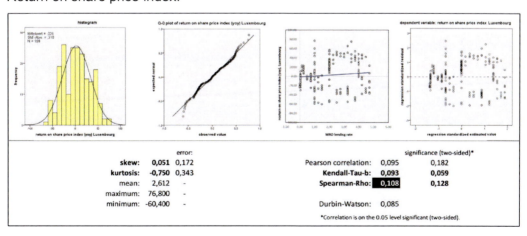

Correlation evaluation of inflation-adjusted interest rates, Luxembourg

Long-term interest rates:

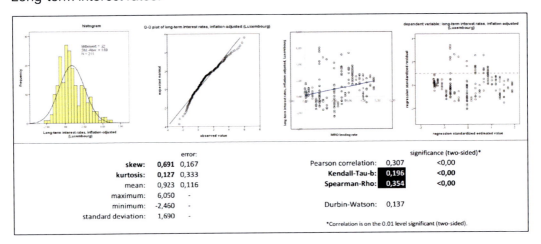

		error:		significance (two-sided)*
skew:	0,691	0,167	Pearson correlation: 0,307	<0,00
kurtosis:	0,127	0,333	Kendall-Tau-b: **0,196**	<0,00
mean:	0,923	0,116	Spearman-Rho: **0,354**	<0,00
maximum:	6,050	-		
minimum:	-2,460	-	Durbin-Watson: 0,137	
standard deviation:	1,690	-	*Correlation is on the 0.01 level significant (two-sided).	

Bank interest rates on deposits:

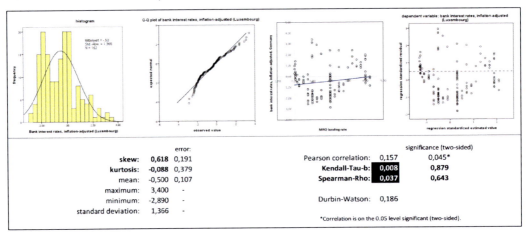

		error:		significance (two-sided)
skew:	0,618	0,191	Pearson correlation: 0,157	0,045*
kurtosis:	-0,088	0,379	Kendall-Tau-b: **0,008**	0,879
mean:	-0,500	0,107	Spearman-Rho: **0,037**	0,643
maximum:	3,400	-		
minimum:	-2,890	-	Durbin-Watson: 0,186	
standard deviation:	1,366	-	*Correlation is on the 0.05 level significant (two-sided).	

Appendix 5:
Development of Nominal Interest Rates vs. Inflation-adjusted Interest Rates

Germany

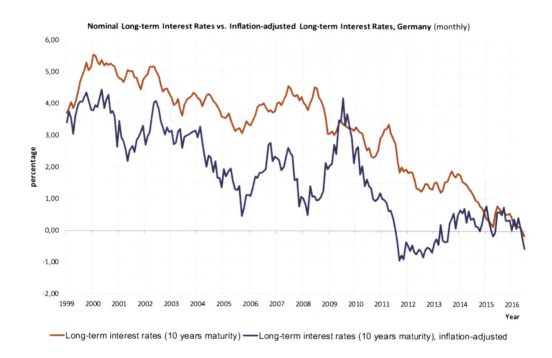

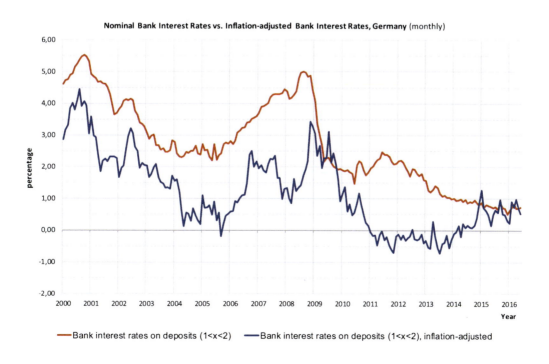

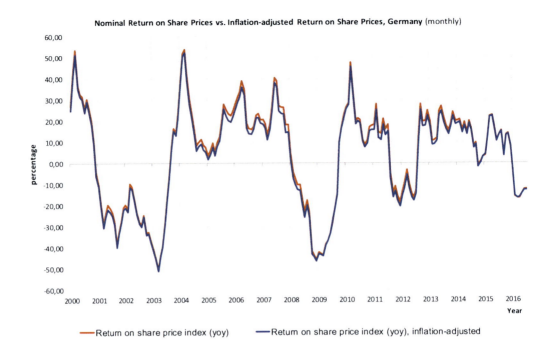

Spain

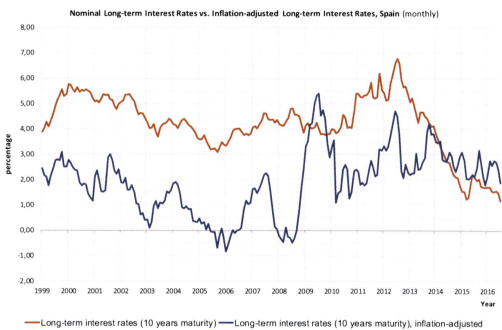

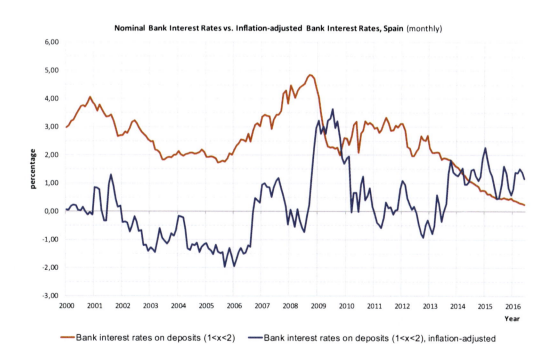

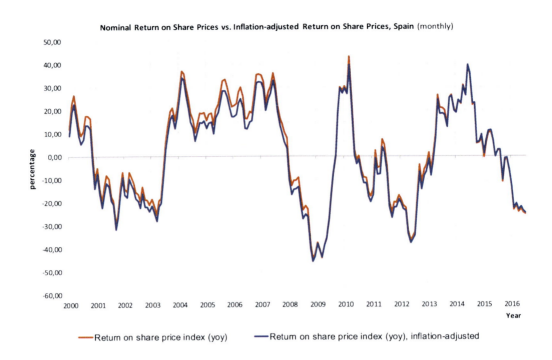

Luxembourg

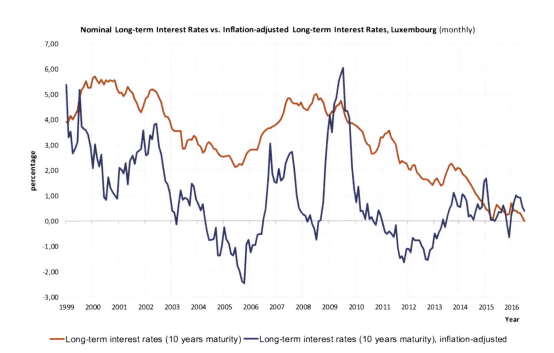

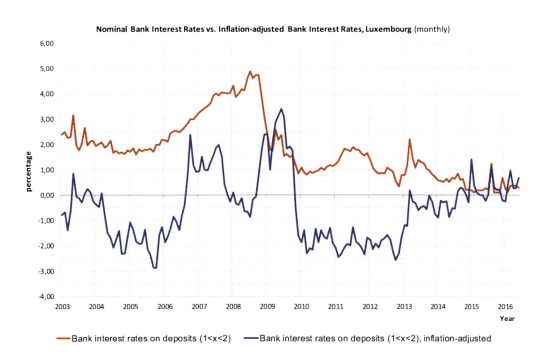

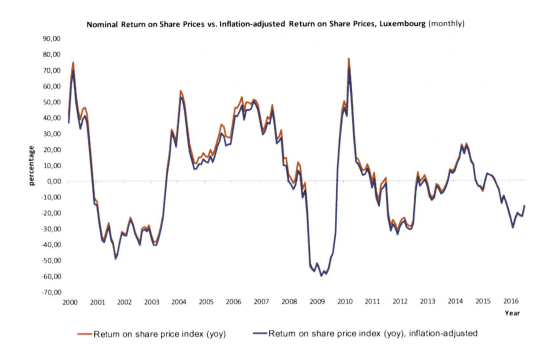